YEADON'S REGISTER

of

LNER

LOCOMOTIVES

ISBN 1 871608 09 0

Published by

IRWELL PRESS

3 Durley Avenue, Pinner, Middlesex, HA5 1JQ.

Printed and bound by Netherwood Dalton & Co., Huddersfield

YEADON'S REGISTER

of

L N E R

LOCOMOTIVES

Volume One

GRESLEY'S A1, A3 Classes

Compiled by

W.B.YEADON

THE REGISTRAR

Born at Yeadon, in the West Riding of Yorkshire, early enough to well remember pre-Grouping liveries, and when even goods engines were cleaned regularly, the railway interest began in 1912 at Shap, and in 1913/14 at Tebay on holidays to visit a relative. Essentially it concentrated on London & North Western locomotives, and remained so based until the middle 1920s. Then, their murder by the Midland and a diversion of interest from locos to lasses, led almost to a cessation of enthusiasm limited to still taking *The Railway Magazine* regularly. After an apprenticeship in mechanical engineering, he had become an A.M.I.Mech.E. in 1930 when his employers in Bradford saw the slump coming and gave a month's notice to 25 out of 35 of their Head Office engineering staff. Fourteen months of unemployment, on the dole of 17 shillings (85p) a week, was terminated by a job which lasted 41 years with a Hull engineering company and meant a move to live in that city, but provided the means to permit marriage in March 1932.

Regarding railway interest, there was then two choices - either study London & North Eastern Railway, or drop it completely. Fortuitously, the L N E R was on the brink of their brilliant 1932-39 period of development. 392 miles of non-stop running was regularly achieved each summer, and on 30th November 1934, *FLYING SCOTSMAN* clocked 100 miles per hour, followed on 5th March 1935 by 2750 *PAPYRUS* reaching a fully authenticated 108 m.p.h. That made any engineer take notice, and already by then, the Registrar had become an L N E R addict. His 55 years and more of meticulous research is now being made available.

INDEX

INTRODUCTION 1
PART ONE—*THE A1 (A10) CLASS* 7
PART TWO—*THE A3 CLASS* 33
PART THREE—*THE A1 CLASS REBUILT TO A3* 49
PART FOUR—*TENDERS* 67
PART FIVE—*SOME MORE DETAIL* 73
PART SIX—*TRIALS & TRIBULATIONS* 83
PART SEVEN—*LIVERIES* 87

Table Indication

LNER	BR.	Pages Nos.
4470	60113	1, 5, 6, 7
4471	60102	6, 7, 12, 47, 60, 82
4472	60103	6, 7, 12, 13, 30, 60
4473	60104	7, 60
4474	60105	8, 11, 14, 17, 60
4475	60106	8, 17, 19; 61
4476	60107	8, 11; 61, 66
4477	60108	8, 18, 63, 83
4478	60109	8, 19, 20, 63
4479	60110	9, 10, 64, 65
4480	60111	10, 48, 64
4481	60112	9, 10, 11, 64, 65, 76, 78, 89
2543	60044	10, 49, 51
2544	60045	10, 48, 49
2545	60046	14, 49
2546	60047	14, 49
2547	60048	14, 26, 50, 87
2548	60049	15, 50
2549	60050	4, 15, 50, 51
2550	60051	15, 50
2551	60052	15, 52, 90
2552	60053	15, 52
2553	60054	16, 52, 78
2554	60055	16, 52
2555	60056	16, 26, 52
2556	60057	16, 53, 81
2557	60058	16, 53
2558	60059	21, 26, 27, 53
2559	60060	21, 28, 29, 53
2560	60061	21, 53
2561	60062	21, 54
2562	60063	21, 54, 79
2563	60064	22, 23, 54
2564	60065	22, 51, 54, 56, 72
2565	60066	22, 55, 59
2566	60067	22, 55
2567	60068	22, 55, 61, 73, 74
2568	60069	23, 24, 55
2569	60070	24, 55
2570	60071	24, 56, 77

Table indication continued

LNER	BR.	Pages Nos.
2571	60072	24, 56, 62
2572	60073	25, 57, 62, 63
2573	60074	25, 46, 57, 66
2574	60075	25, 57, 89
2575	60076	25, 57
2576	60077	25, 58, 80, 81, 89
2577	60078	25, 58
2578	60079	27, 48, 58
2579	60080	4, 27, 58
2580	60081	27, 59, 68
2581	60082	28, 59, 60, 80, 88
2582	60083	28, 86
2743	60089	33, 73
2744	60090	32, 33
2745	60091	33, 69, 88
2746	60092	34
2747	60093	34, 79, 86
2748	60094	34, 37, 88
2749	60095	35, 37
2750	60096	35, 38
2751	60097	35, 84, 86
2752	60098	35, 76
2595	60084	4, 36
2596	60085	36, 38, 68
2597	60086	36
2598	60087	40, 82
2599	60088	40
2795	60099	4, 40, 45
2796	60100	39, 40, 47
2797	60101	39, 41
2500	60035	41, 41
2501	60036	42
2502	60037	43, 87
2503	60038	43, 71
2504	60039	42, 43
2505	60040	43, 71
2506	60041	44, 44, 75
2507	60042	44, 45, 72
2508	60043	45, 46

Numbers in italics indicate a page number of a photograph of that particular locomotive.

Now known and appreciated world-wide as *FLYING SCOTSMAN*, this is how that engine first appeared and ran through 1923 - numbered 1472 and nameless. Here, it is at Ganwick, on a down express between the Hadley Wood North and Potters Bar tunnels.

INTRODUCTION

Nowhere on the L.N.E.R., or on its successor British Railways, was it possible to consult a full history of each locomotive, nor does the Library of the National Railway Museum, or the Public Record Office, yet have such a record available. That came to my attention very clearly in the years from 1955 when I started research to provide basic material for the series of volumes published by the Railway Correspondence & Travel Society dealing with the Locomotives of the L.N.E.R.

This proved understandable when my visits to the many works and offices, enabled me to appreciate just how big a job each had looking after only those locomotives for which they had responsibility. For example, changes of boiler done at Inverurie Works were of scant interest to recording clerks at say, Gorton or Stratford - and vice versa. Nor could those working at Darlington feel deprived when they were not advised of engine movements between sheds in the Scottish Area. I found however, there were sufficient enthusiasts interested enough in having complete coverage and since 1955 I have thus tried to collect, collate, and present this information.

First, it involved obtaining permission to visit workshops, offices and running sheds, to consult such information as each had available. I was able to convince those having authority for this to be granted. No application met with a blunt refusal, and I must here pay tribute to the help I received from those railway executives. Some were puzzled - or sceptical, that there should be such interest, but all were helpful. Amongst those dealing daily with the records of engines still working - much of which was done in handwriting - I came across enthusiasm almost matching my own. Their job gave them a limited picture, covering only engines which directly concerned them. They were intrigued to see how many others in similar jobs would have to be contacted for complete coverage, and how widely spread over England, Scotland and even into Wales I should have to go to do so. To these men, many no higher graded than clerks, do I owe the feasibility of what I have attempted, and such success as I have had.

One unforeseen aspect provided a very positive bonus for me. In 1955 the whole railway thinking was towards *Modernization*, the advent of diesels and the replacement of steam. Diesels needed different recording treatment involving new cards and history sheets. Those for the steam engines were increasingly redundant, so could be made available for me to study. Registers which had been maintained since long before the L.N.E.R. had come into existence had ceased to have currency. One example will suffice to illustrate this. I was given a printed book of Great Northern Railway Engine Stock as at January 1st 1896, which had been up-dated at least three times each year until the end of 1926 i.e. four years into the L.N.E.R's existence. This gift was possible because in the late 1950s such interest as there was in preserving historical relics was mainly targetted on rolling stock, and items of equipment concerned with operating the railways. Interest in gathering archive material was so limited as to be almost negligible. It was further constrained by lack of storage space for dealing with it properly. I still choke at recalling a visit to Darlington Works in the early 1960s, when an official had been instructed to clear a whole room of archives to make way for storage of computer discs. I found, to my horror, that something like twenty tons of paperwork, going back at least forty years, were burned there that week! I located the official in a room where he was more than knee-deep in the contents of filing boxes to be discarded, and was invited to take *such items as I thought of interest*. Two that I was able to rescue will underline the sheer vandalism so thoughtlessly taking place. One was a file of letters from 1924 reporting the re-numbering of former Hull & Barnsley locomotives into the L.N.E.R. series, as they were being done, week by week; a prime example of 'one-off' data. The other was all the correspondence between Gresley, Darlington, and Messrs.Yarrow concerning the development, and progress, of locomotive 10000. For over ten years I took care of this fascinating account, and instead of only the bare bones being available, a fully fleshed description was able to be printed in the RCTS *Part 6C* dealing with the 'Hush-Hush'. Then, in September 1975 when the National Railway Museum opened at York, and included a Library with proper archival facilities, I was able to render unto Caesar the things that belonged to him, (which otherwise would have been destroyed) along with well over five hundredweights of similar material. No wonder my car felt light on the steering on the day I took it to York.

Inevitably, so long as I remained in full time employment, I could not pursue my search for data as diligently as I would have wished. Its location being dispersed as far as 400 miles to the north at Inverurie, 200 miles to the south at Stratford and 100 miles to the west at Gorton meant that I could not often enough be where opportunity knocked, due to time and expense involved. However, it is still with some surprise, and modest satisfaction, that I found so much survived, and surfaced, in order to give you the almost complete account here in Volume 1.

1470, the first of the class, as it went into traffic on 11th April 1922. On the G.N.R. its classification was A1, and this was continued in the L.N.E.R. series, not surprisingly as Doncaster drawing office was responsible for devising it.

EXPLANATION OF CODES AND ABBREVIATIONS USED WITHIN THE TABLES

Throughout the tabulation in this volume a number of codes have been used and to help the reader to understand them, a typical table is set out below with an explanation for each term or code used. The codes will in turn be repeated at the bottom of each relevant page for reference purposes.

The codes used within this volume will not necessarily cover future volumes in this series and so whilst repeating those that are required, new ones will be added, as required.

WORKS CODES

Cow - Cowlairs Works.
Dar - Darlington Works.
Don - Doncaster Works.
Gat - Gateshead Works.
Gor - Gorton Works.
Hay - Haymarket Shed.
Inv - Inverurie Works.
SRX - St Rollox Works.

REPAIR CODES

C/H - Casual Heavy.
C/L - Casual Light.
G - General.
H - Heavy.
H/I - Heavy Intermediate.
L - Light.
L/I - Light Intermediate.
N/C - Non-Classified.

LOCOMOTIVE NUMBER — **2750**   NAME

PAPYRUS

PLACE OF BUILDING — WORKS NUMBER
Doncaster 1708

To traffic 23/3/29   DATE ENTERED TRAFFIC

DATES OUT OF TRAFFIC (Incl)

PLACE OF REPAIR — REPAIRS:
Dar.23/9-24/10/29.**N/C.**
Don.11/4-30/5/30.**G.**   TYPE OF REPAIR

BOILER NUMBER — BOILERS:
8083
8253 (ex2743) 18/11/33   DATE OF ENTRY INTO TRAFFIC WITH THAT BOILER

ORIGIN OF BOILER (first entry as new)

TENDERS:
5273
5331 28/6/29-24/6/32   INCLUSIVE DATES WITH THAT TENDER

TENDER NUMBER

SHEDS:
Kings Cross   DATE TRANSFERRED
Haymarket 14/8/37

RENUMBERED: — DATE RENUMBERED
No.96. 11/11/46

LOCOMOTIVE RUNNING DEPARTMENT

CLASSIFICATION OF REPAIRS

STEAM LOCOMOTIVES

'Heavy' Repairs:-

(a) Engines re-boilered.
(b) Boiler taken out of frame for general repair.
   Any two of the following:-
(c) New tyres fitted to four or more wheels.
(d) Fitting new cylinders.
(e) Fitting new axle or axles, engine or tender.
(f) Re-tubing.
(g) Turning up wheels and re-fitting boxes; or motion and brakework stripped and overhauled.
(h) Boiler repairs in frame with not less than 50 stays renewed.
(The two items in (g) would not in themselves constitute a 'heavy' repair.)

'Light' Repairs:-

(a) Fitting new axle or axles, engine or tender.
(b) Taking out and replace 50 or more boiler tubes.
(c) Taking out and replace four or more superheater flue tubes.
(d) Taking down and replacing superheater header.
(e) Renewal of piston valve liners or piston valves.
(f) Fitting new tyres to one or more wheels.
(g) Turning up four or more wheels and re-fitting boxes.
(h) Complete overhaul of one or more valve gears.
(i) Fitting patch on boiler or fire-box.
(j) Renewing 30 or more firebox stays.
(k) Fitting four or more new axleboxes, or engine axlebox brasses.
(l) Welding, patching, or straightening frame, or renewing buffer beam.
(m) Re-boring cylinders and re-facing ports.
(n) Taking off and repairing tanks.

'OTHER REPAIRS' are those necessitating the engine being out of traffic for 24 hours or over ending midnight and

not coming under 'Heavy' or 'Light'.

The above chart is extracted from form *LNER 3217/5/47 300* issued by the Running Department in 1947 and was to be used when compiling the '*Availability and Use of Steam Engines' Returns.* forms *L.R.7756/1./1a* and /2.

Note: 'Heavy' repairs were frequently entered on Record Cards as 'General'.

Super No. ~~2568~~ 2564 Tender. "*Yagalie*" | Maker *Hyde Park Works.* | 60064 L.R. 7759

EST. 3446 100/7/33

Depôt.			Class.	Type	Built.	Rebuilt.	Brake.	H.A.	Pick-up.	Valves.	Lubricator.
Haymarket 40/3494	4	12 40	~~A1~~ A3	4-6-2	1924/4	—	V	✓	✓	Piston Valve	Wakefield mechanical and Detroit.
Doncaster	3	7 50									

Heavy Repairs.   *Fog Signal Apparatus.*   R-H. DRIVE

Date in.	At.	Booked out.	Back in Traffic.	Remarks.	Special Fittings.
14 9 42	Doncaster	14 11 42		G *Re-classified A3.* G3/43/571.	
2 2 43	Cowlairs.	5		L.	
3 3 44	Doncaster	4 4 44		L.	
12 44		19 12 44		L.	
19 9 45	Doncaster	14 11 45		H.	
8 1 47	"	11 2 47		×G	
13 47		30 1 48		G	
24 5 49	"	9		N	
25 11 50	"	4 1 51		G 81953 ✓	
14 6 51	"	20 6 51		GL	

The mid-morning ritual at Kings Cross termini in the 1920s and 30s with Gresley's unstreamlined Pacifics ready to head the various northbound departures. A3 No.2795 *CALL BOY* starts the procession with the 10 o'clock *FLYING SCOTSMAN*. Also in view are 2549 *PERSIMMON*, 2579 *DICK TURPIN* with 2550 *BLINK BONNY* out of view waiting to back on.

DATES

The dates shown are those taken from the *Engine History Cards*, and are when an engine went into works, and when it was released therefrom. The *Running Department* also kept its own series of record cards, which each shed held for the engines allocated to it. For each works visit their dates were respectively earlier, and later, than the works dates. Shed cards showed the date the engine left for works and, for such as Carlisle or Aberdeen engines going to Doncaster, that could well be at least a couple of days before it reached there. Depending also on the work-load already under repair, an engine could spend one or more days in the yard before it entered the shops. Its journey back to its home shed would also be taken circumspectly, with pauses at sheds en route for examination of bearings. So the time interval on the shed cards always exceeded the period in the works, which is that recorded in this Register. The works dates are used because those are finite, whereas dates of absence from sheds could be subject to appreciable variation with respect to the actual time.

RE-CLASSIFICATION 1945

The seventeen Class A1 surviving in April 1945 were re-classified to Class A10 as and from the 25th April 1945.

NOTICEABLE CHANGES IN APPEARANCE

All A1 class were changed to long travel valves, and this could be discerned in photographs. As A3s in B.R. days they were also changed from right-hand to left-hand drive. Later, double chimney, and trough smoke deflectors were significant additions. Dates for these changes are all included in *Part 2A of Locomotives of the LNER*, published by *The Railway Correspondence and Travel Society*, to which those interested are referred, and to which the author made a significant contribution.

TENDER CHANGES

Where dates have a gap of some 3 or 4 weeks, the engine was in the works, and had been detached from the tender it had brought in, and which it would not necessarily take out on completion of that repair. Where the dates coincide - or differ by only a day or so - that indicates the change was made almost surely at the engine's home shed.

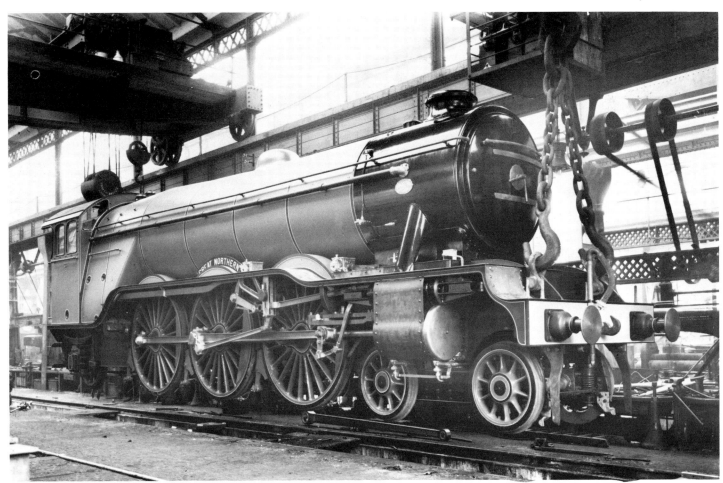

No.1470 *GREAT NORTHERN* being lifted off the pit at Doncaster Works on the 24th March 1922. Gresley's first Pacific is virtually ready to start setting new records and make history.

National Railway Museum

1470 at New Southgate taking the 4 o'clock from Kings Cross as far as Doncaster where it was shedded. Note square corners to front buffer beam and no front footsteps fitted.

4472 spent most of 1924 and 1925 as the LNER prestige exhibit at the British Empire Exhibition at Wembley, for which the cab sides carried the Company's coat-of-arms, seen here during 1926 in the locomotive yard at Kings Cross station. It still had square corners to its buffer beam and the redundant second lamp iron above the nearside buffer.

When climbing to Potters Bar summit, as this 1935 view clearly shows, there was no need for smoke deflectors. 4471 has now had its cab and boiler mountings reduced in height, buffer beam lower corner clearances increased, and a redundant second lamp iron removed.

PART ONE

THE A1 (A10) CLASS

Repairs:-	**C/H**-Casual Heavy.	**C/L**-Casual Light.	**G**-General.	**H**-Heavy.	**H/I**-Heavy Intermediate.	**L**-Light.	**L/I**-Light Intermediate.	**N/C**-Non-Classified.
Works:-	Cow - Cowlairs.	Dar - Darlington.	Don - Doncaster.	Gat - Gateshead.	Gor - Gorton.	Hay - Haymarket shed.	SRX - St Rollox.	

1470
GREAT NORTHERN

DONCASTER 1536

To traffic 11/4/22

REPAIRS:
Don.27-29/9/22.**N/C.**
Don.24-26/10/22.**L.**
Don.4-6/12/22.**L.**
Don.1-2/1/23.**L.**
Don.23-29/1/23.**L.**
Don.3-8/2/23.**L.**
Don.23-26/5/23.**L.**
Don.22/8-9/10/23.**H.**
Don.28/2-9/4/24.**H.**
Don.1/12/24-21/3/25.**G.**
Don.16-18/4/25.**L.**
Don.1-6/2/26.**L.**
Don.3-8/6/26.**L.**
Don.4/3-30/4/27.**G.**
Don.29/3-8/6/28.**G.**
Don.25-30/10/28.**L.**
Don.7/5-29/6/29.**G.**
Don.10/6-2/8/30.**G.**
Don.24/10-12/11/30.**L.**
Don.23/9-12/12/31.**G.**
Don.6/4-25/5/33.**G.**
Don.29/12/33-8/2/34.**H.**
Don.29/11/34-16/1/35.**G.**
Don.5/3-22/4/36.**H.**
Don.15/1-27/2/37.**G.**
Don.29/11-2/12/37.**L.**
Blow-down Apparatus.
Don.2/3-2/4/38.**G.**
Don.17/4-20/5/39.**G.**
Don.5-30/3/40.**G.**
Don.8/1-14/2/42.**G.**
Don.20/11-24/12/43.**G.**
Don.1/5/45- *Into shops for rebuilding to Class A1/1. Subsequent history to be found in Vol.3.*

BOILERS:
7646
7783 (new) 30/4/27
7765 (ex4478) 2/8/30
7646 (ex4478) 25/5/33
7774 (ex2551) 27/2/37
7767 (ex2557) 30/3/40

TENDERS:
5211 11/4/22-29/3/28
5227 8/6/28-15/1/37
5582 27/2/37-

SHEDS:
Doncaster
Gorton 8/7/44
Kings Cross 29/10/44
Doncaster 11/11/44

RENUMBERED:
1470N. 9/10/23.
4470. 21/3/25

1471
SIR FREDERICK BANBURY

DONCASTER 1539

To traffic 10/7/22

REPAIRS:
Don.14-21/8/22.**N/C.**
'Indicator' gear fitted.
Don.30/10-4/11/22.**L.**
Don.9-10/11/22.*Naming.*
Don.3-10/3/23.**L.**
Don.10/8/23.**N/C.**
Don.12/10-14/12/23.**G.**
Don.23-31/1/24.**L.**
Don.7/7/24.**L.**
Don.20/10-6/11/24.**H.**
Don.17/4-1/8/25.**G.**
Don.22/1-6/2/26.**L.**
Don.25/2-20/3/26.**L.**
Don.19/5-19/6/26.**L.**
Don.22/3-18/6/27.**L.**
Don.26-29/10/27.**L.**
Don.21/12/27-13/3/28.**H.**
Don.2/10-28/11/28.**G.**
Don.9/5-17/7/29.**H.**
Don.24/9-27/11/30.**G.**
Don.29/9-20/11/31.**H.**
Don.3/2-1/4/33.**H.**
Don.28/9-2/11/34.**G.**
Don.31/1-20/3/36.**G.**
Don.2/4-8/5/37.**G.**
Don.23-25/11/37.**L.**
Blow-down Apparatus
Don.13/4-27/5/38.**G.**
Don.12-20/9/38.**L.**
Water Scoop Altered
Don.26/6-12/8/39.**G.**
Don.18/2-22/3/41.**G.**
Don.8/9/42- *Into shops for rebuilding to Class A3*

BOILERS:
7647
7879 (new) 18/6/27
7772 (ex2554) 27/11/30
7767 (ex2566) 2/11/34
7790 (ex2570) 27/5/38

TENDERS:
5212 10/7/22-8/9/42

SHEDS:
Doncaster
Grantham 12/12/32
Doncaster 5/5/33

RENUMBERED:
No.1471N. 14/12/23
No.4471. 1/8/25

1472
FLYING SCOTSMAN

DONCASTER 1564

To traffic 24/2/23

REPAIRS:
Don.27/12/23-2/3/24.**G.**
Prepared for Wembley Exhibition.
Don.23/3-19/4/25.**H.**
K3 tender coupled.
Don.16-28/11/25.**L.**
Own tender replaced.
Don.18/2-28/4/27.**G.**
Variable blastpipe on.
Don.14/2-5/4/28.**G.**
Don.23/4-8/6/29.**G.**
Don.17/1-15/3/30.**G.**
Don.10/2-2/4/31.**G.**
Don.6/4-20/5/32.**G.**
Don.23/2-27/4/33.**G.**
Don.19/4-30/5/34.**G.**
Don.26-27/11/34.**L.**
Don.27/3-18/5/35.**G.**
Don.25/3-14/6/36.**H.**
Don.19-20/10/36.**N/C.**
Corridor tender removed.
Don.25/6-24/7/37.**G.**
Don.12-13/4/38.**L.**
Don.27/5-2/7/38.**G.**
Don.18/9-3/11/39.**G.**
Don.20-23/11/39.**L.**
Blow-down Apparatus.
Don.10/5-11/6/41.**G.**
Don.27/2-3/4/43.**G.**
Don.5-23/2/44.**L.**
Don.3/2-10/3/45.**G.**
Don.18/5/46.**L.**
Don.18/11/46- *Into shops for rebuilding to Class A3.*

BOILERS:
7693
7878 (new) 5/4/28
7804 (ex2581) 27/4/33
7772 (ex4471) 18/5/35
7785 (ex2561) 3/11/39

TENDERS:
5223 24/2/23-19/4/25
5378 19/4/25-16/11/25.
K3 tender
5223 16/11/25-14/2/28
5323 5/4/28-23/4/29
5324 8/6/29-19/10/36
5290 20/10/36-27/5/38

5640 2/7/38-

SHEDS:
Doncaster
Kings Cross 11/4/28
Doncaster 6/3/39
New England 12/3/44
Gorton 7/7/44
Kings Cross 29/10/44
New England 11/11/44
Doncaster 5/12/44

RENUMBERED:
No.4472 2/3/24
No.502 20/1/46
No.103 5/5/46

1473
SOLARIO

DONCASTER 1565

To traffic 17/3/23

REPAIRS:
Don.21-25/9/23.**L.**
Don.7/4-14/6/24.**G.**
Don.16-19/7/24.**L.**
Don.7-14/10/24.**L.**
Don.23/10/25-30/1/26.**G.**
Don.24/9-16/10/26.**L.**
Don.12/10-15/12/27.**G.**
Don.3-6/2/28.**L.**
Don.17/7-7/9/28.**H.**
Don.5/9-26/10/29.**G.**
Don.6-17/5/30.**L.**
Don.28/1-1/4/31.**G.**
Don.12/4-7/6/32.**G.**
Don.30/12/32-9/3/33.**H.**
Don.16/5-8/7/33.**G.**
Don.27/9-1/11/34.**G.**
Don.10/2-2/4/36.**G.**
Don.9-12/11/36.**L.**
Don.5/5-18/6/37.**G.**
Don.10-13/11/37.**L.**
Blow-down Apparatus.
Don.23/9-31/10/38.**G.**
Don.1/8-22/9/39.**H.**
Don.22/8/41- *Into shops for rebuilding to Class A3.*

BOILERS:
7694
7646 (ex4470) 15/12/27
7701 (ex2558) 26/10/29
7792 (ex2574) 7/6/32
7647 (ex4479) 1/11/34
7700 (ex4474) 2/4/36

TENDERS:
5224 17/3/23-3/3/29
5254 4/3/29-

SHEDS:
Doncaster
Copley Hill 25/9/37
Doncaster 9/11/37
Copley Hill 18/11/37
Doncaster 3/1/38
Gorton 1/5/39

RENUMBERED:
No.4473. 14/6/24

This may have been 1473N from 25/9/23 but no evidence has been found.

1474
VICTOR WILD

DONCASTER   1566

To traffic 24/3/23

REPAIRS:
Don.4-14/12/23.**L.**
Don.16/9-15/11/24.**G.**
Don.13/3-19/6/26.**G.**
Don.21/2-1/3/27.**L.**
Don.9-27/6/27.**L.**
Don.10/1-19/5/28.**G.**
Don.14/8-30/9/29.**G.**
Don.11/11/30-9/1/31.**G.**
Don.14/1-5/3/32.**G.**
Don.13/4-13/5/32.**L.**
Don.25/11/32-13/1/33.**H.**
Don.11/12/33-6/2/34.**G.**
Don.1/6-13/7/35.**G.**
Don.25/6-1/8/36.**G.**
Don.18/8-2/10/37.**G.**
Don.9-10/11/37.**L.**
Blow-down Apparatus.
Don.5/11-16/12/38.**G.**
Don.9/11-19/12/40.**G.**
Don.10/8/42- *Into shops for rebuilding to Class A3.*

BOILERS:
7695
7700 (ex4479) 30/9/29
7804 (ex4472) 13/7/35
7646 (ex4470) 2/10/37

TENDERS:
5225 24/3/23-10/7/33
5327 10/7/33-24/8/34
5225 24/8/34-4/9/34
5329 4/9/34-15/9/34
5225 15/9/34-

SHEDS:
Kings Cross
Doncaster 5/1/37
Gorton 25/2/39
Leicester Cen. 19/8/39
Gorton 2/12/39

RENUMBERED:
No.1474N. 14/12/23
No.4474. 15/11/24

1475
FLYING FOX

DONCASTER   1567

To traffic 28/4/23

REPAIRS:
Don.27/11/24-14/2/25.**G.**
Don.7/11/25-6/2/26.**G.**
Don.21/4-4/6/27.**G.**
Don.11-13/6/27.**N/C.**
Don.2/6-24/7/28.**G.**
Don.12/2-13/4/29.**L.**
Don.1/1-1/3/30.**G.**
Don.13-17/5/30.**L.**
Don.28/11/30-31/1/31.**G.**
Don.12/6-6/7/31.**L.**
Don.21/3-27/5/32.**G.**
Don.11/5-1/7/33.**G.**
Don.23/4-8/6/34.**G.**
Don.25/4-13/6/35.**G.**
Don.17-19/10/35.**L.**
Don.22/4-10/6/36.**G.**
Don.23-29/10/36.**L.**
Corridor tender removed.
Don.2/2-18/3/37.**G.**
Don.29/12/37-29/1/38.**G.**
Don.17/2-1/4/39.**G.**
Don.6/5-8/6/40.**G.**
Don.29/12/41-6/2/42.**G.**
Don.13/10-5/11/43.**G.**
Don.2/6-21/7/45.**G.**
Don.28/1/47- *Into shops for rebuilding to Class A3.*

BOILERS:
7696
7699 (ex4478) 24/7/28
7878 (ex4472) 1/7/33
7768 (ex2556) 18/3/37
7779 (ex4481) 8/6/40
7767 (ex4470) 21/7/45

TENDERS:
5226 28/4/23-2/6/28
5228 21/7/28-10/8/28
5329 10/8/28-4/9/34
5225 4/9/34-15/9/34
5329 15/9/34-25/4/35
5323 13/6/35-23/10/36
5483 29/10/36-2/2/37
5279 18/3/37-6/5/40
5278 8/6/40-

SHEDS:
Kings Cross
New England 26/6/40
Grantham 4/4/44
Kings Cross 16/4/44
Gorton 9/7/44
Kings Cross 29/10/44
Copley Hill 6/12/44
New England 22/1/45

RENUMBERED:
No.4475. 14/2/25
No.106. 29/5/46

1476
ROYAL LANCER

DONCASTER   1568

To traffic 26/5/23

REPAIRS:
Don.26/5-14/6/24.**L.**
Don.27/11/24-7/2/25.**G.**
Don.17/4-22/7/26.**G.**
Don.14/1-9/2/27.**H.**
Don.23/12/27-5/4/28.**G.**
Don.17/4-25/5/29.**G.**
Don.18/3-16/5/30.**G.**
Don.20/3-9/5/31.**G.**
Don.7/12/31-4/2/32.**H.**
Don.3-18/6/32.**H.**
Don.28/4-5/7/33.**G.**
Don.25/5-30/6/34.**G.**
Don.18-22/12/34.**L.**
Don.15/5-27/6/35.**G.**
Don.9-14/3/36.**L.**
Don.7/5-19/6/36.**G.**
Don.9/6-10/7/37.**G.**
Don.13/4-16/5/38.**G.**
Don.25/11-5/12/38.**L.**
Don.30/6-19/8/39.**G.**
Don.27/2-13/3/40.**L.**
Don.17/5-3/6/40.**L.**
Don.2/5-6/6/41.**G.**
Don.23/1-20/2/43.**G.**
Don.27/7-4/9/43.**L.**
Don.1/11-16/12/44.**G.**
Don.29/11-30/12/45.**L.**
Don.10/8/46- *Into shops for rebuilding to Class A3.*

BOILERS:
7697
7647 (ex4471) 5/4/28
7793 (ex2577) 9/5/31
7702 (ex4481) 27/6/35
7701 (ex4478/ 19/8/39

TENDERS:
5227 26/5/23-23/12/27
5324 5/4/28-17/4/29
5323 25/5/29-15/5/35
5329 27/6/35-9/6/37
5481 10/7/37-23/1/43
5267 20/2/43-

SHEDS:
Grantham
Kings Cross 11/4/28
New England 26/6/40
Grantham 11/4/44
New England 11/6/44
Gorton 7/7/44
Kings Cross 29/10/44
Grantham 16/12/44
Kings Cross 19/5/46

RENUMBERED:
No.4476. 7/2/25

1477
GAY CRUSADER

DONCASTER   1569

To traffic 16/6/23

REPAIRS:
Don.8-9/8/23.**N/C.**

Don.24/8-25/9/23.**L.**
Don.19-22/12/23.**L.**
Don.5-7/6/24.**L.**
Don.10/3-20/6/25.**G.**
Don.18-23/2/26.**L.**
Valve gear modifications.
Don.19/1-9/4/27.**G.**
Don.27/10-3/11/27.**L.**
'Diamond' soot blower fitted.
Don.30/1/28.**L.**
Don.6-10/2/28.**L.**
Don.17/4-13/6/28.**G.**
Don.19-23/10/28.**L.**
Don.7/10-30/11/29.**G.**
Don.19/6-12/7/30.**L.**
Don.1/12/30-14/2/31.**G.**
Don.20/4-11/6/32.**G.**
Don.12/8-27/9/33.**G.**
Don.1-19/12/33.**L.**
Don.6/2-7/3/35.**G.**
Don.9-11/4/35.**L.**
Don.17/1-5/3/36.**G.**
Don.7-8/4/36.**L.**
Don.20-28/11/36.**H.**
Don.14/5-23/6/37.**G.**
Don.4/11/37.**L.**
Blow-down apparatus.
Don.9/6-22/7/38.**G.**
Don.25/9-11/11/39.**G.**
Don.1-31/5/41.**G.**
Don.22/12/42- *Into shops for rebuilding to Class A3.*

BOILERS:
7698
7704 (ex2544) 13/6/28
7703 (ex2543) 30/11/29
7765 (ex4470) 27/9/33
7697 (ex4479) 23/6/37

TENDERS:
5228 16/6/23-17/4/28
5211 13/6/28-14/5/37
5266 23/6/37-

SHEDS:
Doncaster
Grantham 12/11/34
Doncaster 11/4/35
Gorton 7/12/41

RENUMBERED:
No.1477N. 25/9/23
No.4477. 20/6/25

1478
HERMIT

DONCASTER   1570

To traffic 30/6/23

REPAIRS:
Don.25-26/9/23.**L.**
Don.14-15/11/23.**L.**
Don.8-17/11/24.**L.**
Don.8/12/24-5/3/25.**G.**
Don.21/10-14/11/25.**L.**
Don.17-23/7/26.**L.**
Don.2/11/26-19/1/27.**G.**
Don.4-16/7/27.**H.**

Repairs:- **C/H**-Casual Heavy.   **C/L**-Casual Light.   **G**-General.   **H**-Heavy.   **H/I**-Heavy Intermediate.   **L**-Light.   **L/I**-Light Intermediate.   **N/C**-Non-Classified.
Works:-   **Cow** - Cowlairs.   **Dar** - Darlington.   **Don** - Doncaster.   **Gat** - Gateshead.   **Gor** - Gorton.   **Hay** - Haymarket shed.   **SRX** - St Rollox.

The lack of turning facilities at Kings Cross led to their only being allocated two out of the ten Pacifics built in 1923. Doncaster got five, and the other three went to Grantham shed. 1479 was one of the Grantham engines (the others were 1476 and 1480) and they were used more often on northbound trains to York rather than southbound workings to London in early LNER years. 1479 here has just left York with the 10.20 a.m. Newcastle to Kings Cross restaurant car express. It was new 25th July 1923 and had the 'N' suffix added ex works 19th October 1923.

The last of the first batch was to traffic on 8th September 1923 as 1481N, and here on a down express is passing what was left of Oakleigh Park down signalbox. It differed significantly from the preceding eleven Pacifics in that the heights of the boiler mountings and cab roof had been reduced to permit working other than just on the G.N. main line. Gateshead shed had the use of it from November 1923 until April 1924 when it returned south to Doncaster shed. Whilst on the North Eastern Area it was found that the overhang at the front tended to argue with the platform edge of the curved entry into Newcastle Central and so 1481N went into Gateshead Works to have its bar iron front footsteps removed and to get incurved lower corners to its buffer beam, as shown in this picture.

Don.9/11/27-5/3/28.**G.**
Don.18/6-4/7/28.**L.**
Don.3/12/28-23/2/29.**G.**
Don.13/2-12/4/30.**G.**
Don.9/2-11/4/31.**G.**
Don.27/5-9/6/31.**L.**
Don.18/12/31-17/2/32.**G.**
Don.5/1-7/3/33.**G.**
Don.16/6-27/7/34.**G.**
Don.13/6-19/7/35.**G.**
Don.6/7-21/8/36.**G.**
Don.7/12/36-16/1/37.**G.**
Don.29/12/37-26/1/38.**G.**
Don.16/8-24/9/38.**H.**
Don.19/2-5/4/40.**G.**
Don.22/1-7/3/42.**G.**
Don.4/10/43- *Into shops for rebuilding to Class A3.*

BOILERS:
7699
7765 (ex2547) 5/3/28
7646 (ex4473) 12/4/30
7701 (ex4473) 7/3/33
7791 (ex2404) 26/1/38

TENDERS:
5229 30/6/23-27/3/32
5259 27/3/32-19/2/40
5289 5/4/40-

SHEDS:
Doncaster
Grantham 16/9/28
Doncaster 26/4/38
Gorton 4/3/39
Kings Cross 22/11/42
Copley Hill 15/2/43
Doncaster 28/9/43

RENUMBERED:
No.1478N. 26/9/23
No.4478. 5/3/25

1479
ROBERT THE DEVIL

DONCASTER 1571

To traffic 25/7/23

REPAIRS:
Don.4-9/8/23.**N/C.**
Don.17-19/10/23.**N/C.**
Don.11-13/12/23.**L.**
Don.26/3-7/4/24.**L.**
Don.2-9/6/24.**L.**
Don.1-11/10/24.**H.**
Don.5/1-11/4/25.**G.**
Don.16/2-5/6/26.**G.**
Don.21/3-18/6/27.**G.**
Don.21/10-14/11/27.**H.**
Don.7-31/3/28.**L.**
Don.17/12/28-4/3/29.**G.**
Don.6/12/29-20/2/30.**G.**
Don.20/10-16/12/30.**H.**
Don.20/10-3/12/31.**G.**
Don.12-2-23/3/32.**L.**
Don.7/2-8/4/33.**G.**
Don.30/9-16/11/33.**H.**
Don.16/8-19/9/34.**G.**
Don.8-16/4/35.**L.**

Don.5/9-25/10/35.**G.**
Don.8/10-18/11/36.**G.**
Don.28/12/37-3/2/38.**G.**
Don.5-11/4/38.**L.**
Don.18-21/7/38.**L.**
Don.14/4-20/5/39.**G.**
Don.5/9-19/10/40.**G.**
Don.9/7/42- *Into shops for rebuilding to Class A3.*

BOILERS:
7700
7697 (ex4476) 4/3/29
7647 (ex4476) 3/12/31
7697 (ex2579) 19/9/34
7795 (ex2545) 18/11/36
7776 (ex2546) 19/10/40

TENDERS:
5230 25/7/23-

SHEDS:
Grantham
New England 7/1/42

RENUMBERED:
No.1479N. 19/10/23
No.4479. 11/4/25

1480
ENTERPRISE

DONCASTER 1572

To traffic 17/8/23

REPAIRS:
Don.24-25/8/23.**N/C.**
Don.7-12/1/24.**N/C.**
Don.14/1-11/4/25.**G.**
Don.21/4-31/7/26.**G.**
Don.15-18/1/27.**L.**
Don.9/5/27- *Into shops for rebuilding to Class A3.*

BOILERS:
7701

TENDERS:
5231 17/8/23-

SHEDS:
Grantham

RENUMBERED:
No.1480N. 25/8/23
No.4480. 11/4/25

1481N
ST SIMON

DONCASTER 1573

To traffic 8/9/23

REPAIRS:
Don.4-6/10/23.**L.**
Dar.1-13/11/23.**L.**
Raven F.S.A. fitted.
Gat.5/12/23-10/1/24.**L.**
Don.28/4-1/8/25.**G.**

Dar.18/8-20/10/25.**L.**
Don.7-26/12/25.**L.**
Don.4-14/8/26.**L.**
Don.18/12/26-7/1/27.**L.**
Don.7/4-2/7/27.**G.**
Don.22-25/8/27.**L.**
Don.23/4-16/6/28.**G.**
Don.28/10-24/12/29.**G.**
Don.27/11/30-24/1/31.**G.**
Don.3/3/-6/5/32.**G.**
Don.28/4-24/6/33.**G.**
Don.12-13/7/34.**L.**
Don.1/11-13/12/34.**G.**
Don.17/2-16/4/36.**G.**
Don.5-8/5/36.**L.**
Don.14/4-15/5/37.**G.**
Don.22-23/10/37.**L.**
Blow-down apparatus.
Don.8-12/4/38.**L.**
Don.7/5-15/6/38.**G.**
Don.25/7-1/9/39.**G.**
Don.17/10-13/11/40.**L.**
Don.3/2-19/3/41.**G.**
Don.25/1-19/2/43.**G.**
Don.2/11-21/12/44.**G.**
Don.6/7/46- *Into shops for rebuilding to Class A3.*

BOILERS:
7702
7694 (ex4473) 16/6/28
7693 (ex2543) 24/1/31
7702 (ex2563) 24/6/33
7779 (ex2393) 13/12/34
7784 (ex2579) 1/9/39

TENDERS:
5232 8/9/23-14/4/37
5643 15/5/37-8/4/38
5280 12/4/38-7/5/38
5223 7/5/38-

SHEDS:
Doncaster
Gateshead 1/11/23
Doncaster 10/4/24
New England 4/11/27
Doncaster 8/11/27
Grantham 17/2/31
Doncaster 21/2/31
Copley Hill 3/12/43
Doncaster 29/5/44
Grantham 28/10/45
Kings Cross 19/5/46

RENUMBERED:
No.4481. 1/8/25
No.511. 20/1/46
No.112. 11/5/46

2543
MELTON

DONCASTER 1598

To traffic 28/6/24

REPAIRS:
Don.4-9/8/24.**L.**
Don.4/11/25-20/2/26.**G.**
Don.26/4-25/6/27.**G.**

Don.23/2-31/5/28.**H.**
Don.17/4-1/6/29.**G.**
Don.30/10-29/12/30.**G.**
Don.28/1-15/3/32.**G.**
Don.12/7/32.**L.**
Wheel spoke welding.
Don.21/2/33.**L.**
Wheel spoke welding.
Don.28/4-21/6/33.**G.**
Don.6/9-13/10/34.**G.**
Don.18/9-1/11/35.**G.**
Don.8/1-20/2/37.**G.**
Don.26-27/10/37.**L.**
Blow-down apparatus.
Don.8/7-5/8/38.**L.**
Don.9/6-21/7/39.**G.**
Don.30/12/40-15/2/41.**G.**
Don.5/11-9/12/42.**G.**
Don.1-16/1/44.**L.**
Don.9/5-14/6/44.**G.**
Don.9/1-16/2/46.**G.**
Don.22/7/47- *Into shops for rebuilding to Class A3.*

BOILERS:
7703
7693 (ex4472) 1/6/29
7783 (ex4470) 29/12/30
7789 (ex2566) 21/6/33
7766 (ex2577) 1/11/35
7879 (ex2576) 15/2/41
7797 (ex2565) 16/2/46

TENDERS:
5253 28/6/24-26/3/29
5269 26/3/29-17/4/29
5224 1/6/29-8/7/38
5580 5/8/38-

SHEDS:
Grantham
Doncaster 21/8/24
Gorton 1/9/24
Doncaster 8/9/24
Kings Cross 4/3/27
Doncaster 20/3/27
Grantham 19/1/30
Kings Cross 11/3/30
Doncaster 12/6/30
New England 12/3/44
Kings Cross 24/9/44
Copley Hill 6/12/44
New England 22/1/45

RENUMBERED:
No.44. 1/9/46

2544
LEMBERG

DONCASTER 1600

To traffic 26/7/24

REPAIRS:
Don.5-15/8/25.**L.**
Don.12/10-31/12/25.**G.**
Don.4-9/10/26.**L.**
Don.8-17/8/27.**L.**
Don.8/9/27- *Into shops for rebuilding to Class A3.*

Repairs:- **C/H**-Casual Heavy.   **C/L**-Casual Light.   **G**-General.   **H**-Heavy.   **H/I**-Heavy Intermediate.   **L**-Light.   **L/I**-Light Intermediate.   **N/C**-Non-Classified.
Works:-   Cow - Cowlairs.   Dar - Darlington.   Don - Doncaster.   Gat - Gateshead.   Gor - Gorton.   Hay - Haymarket shed.   SRX - St Rollox.

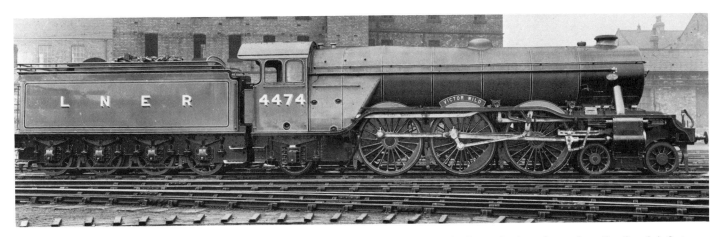

When the corridor tender was introduced in 1928, it was recognised that occasions would arise for them to be changed to engines other than their first coupling. In consequence, they carried only *L N E R* but in 12″ instead of 7½″, and the engine number was moved to the cab side. 4474 did not have a corridor tender until July 1933; with the engine ex works on 19th May 1928, this photograph was taken to show the effect of the change on tenders other than the corridor type. It proved acceptable, and the cab number became standard.

4476 from 27th June 1935 was the first to have the cab sides altered to smaller cut-out and longer vertical handrail, consequent on the fitting of bucket type seats for the crew.

1481N was the first one adapted for operating other than on the Great Northern main line which had a more generous loading gauge than some of the other L.N.E.R. routes, particularly the North British. So that it could work to Edinburgh, the cab roof height above the footplate was made almost 6″ lower, but the ventilator in the centre did not need any alteration, and so always remained a prominent feature.

Seen here at York, 4472 is accelerating the down non-stop after slowing for the passage of the long curved station. It is a great regret that the date of this picture has not been discovered because on no other occasion was 4472 seen in traffic, and particularly on a non-stop, when improperly dressed i.e. running anonymously. The original set of nameplates put on the A1 class proved prone to cracking, and were duly replaced.

4472 worked from Doncaster shed from new until early 1928, to and from London on heavy expresses. Note the short nameplates and their position back from the splasher face.

It was not until July 1930 that Pacifics were allowed to work between Doncaster and Leeds (Central) and another six years before they did so regularly. Then Doncaster shed sent Nos.2553 and 2555 to Leeds Copley Hill shed, mainly to work the 'Queen of Scots' Pullman trains to and from London. Here at the Leeds shed in May 1939, No.4471 is deputising for 2555 which was away at works for a general repair.

The replacement nameplates were not only stronger, but also longer as seen here in a 1935 photo of 4472, and they were fitted nearer to the face of the splasher. Now their ends came almost to running plate level. This view also shows the reduction in the cab cut-out consequent on the fitting of bucket-type seats for the driver and fireman.

Gresley's development of his Pacific design, through the A3 class improvements to the superb A4 class, made A1s redundant for the non-stop workings, so they relinquished the corridor tenders. Although 4472 lost its tender in October 1936, and reverted to the G.N.design with coal rails until May 1938, it was then a high-sided non-corridor type which had a built-up front end similar to those with corridor. Here picking up water from Werrington troughs, it is on the 'Queen of Scots' Pullman from London to Leeds (Central).

Until almost the end of 1923, when the required 70 foot turntable was put in, Pacifics could not be turned at Kings Cross, and they had to run light engine to and from the table at Ferme Park opposite Hornsey shed, a wasted trip of eight miles. Here 1474 is using that table in 1923.

2544 continued

BOILERS:
7704

TENDERS:
5254 26/7/24-

SHEDS:
Gorton
Doncaster 27/8/24

2545
DIAMOND JUBILEE

DONCASTER   1601

To traffic 9/8/24

REPAIRS:
Don.20/2-29/5/26.**G.**
Don.14/3-29/4/27.**G.**
Don.2-7/7/27.**L.**
Don.12/3-6/6/28.**G.**
Don.24/5-17/7/29.**G.**
Don.30/1-15/3/30.**G.**
Don.6/3-9/5/31.**G.**
Don.1/4-28/5/32.**G.**
Don.2/2-23/3/33.**G.**
Don.5-31/10/33.**L.**
Don.28/5-7/7/34.**G.**
Don.28/5-6/7/35.**G.**
Don.11/6-23/7/36.**G.**
Don.27/4-12/6/37.**G.**
Don.19/9-22/10/38.**G.**
Don.3-6/1/39.**L.**
Blow-down apparatus and rub-

ber fairing put on.
Don.8/1-24/2/40.**G.**
Don.26/11-17/1/41.
Don.3/7/41- *Into shops for rebuilding to Class A3.*

BOILERS:
7763
7778 (ex2560) 9/5/31
7795 (ex2576) 23/3/33
7703 (ex2550) 23/7/36

TENDERS:
5255 9/8/24-12/3/28
5266 6/6/28-27/4/37
5644 12/6/37-

SHEDS:
Gorton
Kings Cross 3/9/24
Grantham 7/6/28

2546
DONOVAN

DONCASTER   1602

To traffic 30/8/24

REPAIRS:
Don.3/10/25-2/1/26.**G.**
Don.21/2-5/3/27.**L.**
Don.9-16/7/27.**L.**
Don.13/10-23/12/27.**G.**
Don.21/2-22/4/29.**G.**
Don.11/3-2/5/30.**G.**
Don.13/4-2/6/31.**G.**
Don.26/8-18/10/32.**G.**

Don.6/7-11/8/33.**G.**
Don.27/9-25/10/34.**G.**
Don.26/11-35-17/1/36.**G.**
Don.16/3-1/5/37.**G.**
Don.22/4-2/6/38.**G.**
Don.14-23/11/38.**L.**
Don.24/4-16/6/39.**G.**
Don.28/1-8/3/41.**G.**
Don.22/4-1/5/41.**L.**
Don.9/11-18/12/42.**G.**
Don.17/6-26/7/44.**G.**
Don.25/4-5/5/45.**L.**
Don.9/3-27/4/46.**G.**
Don.1/12/47- *Into shops for rebuilding to Class A3.*

BOILERS:
7764
7704 (ex4477) 2/5/30
7776 (ex2556) 25/10/34
7804 (ex4474) 16/6/39

TENDERS:
5256 30/8/24-2/5/28
5327 2/5/28-6/5/28
5256 6/5/28-22/4/38
5269 2/6/38-17/6/44
5284 26/7/44-

SHEDS:
Kings Cross
Grantham 1/6/28
Kings Cross 7/6/28
Neasden 30/6/39
Gorton 23/2/41
Kings Cross 18/12/42
Gorton 26/7/44

Kings Cross 29/10/44
Copley Hill 17/12/44
Doncaster 22/1/45
Grantham 28/10/45
Kings Cross 19/5/46

RENUMBERED:
No.47. 17/9/46

2547
DONCASTER

DONCASTER   1603

To traffic 30/8/24

REPAIRS:
Don.2-8/1/25.**L.**
Don.22/5-3/6/25.**L.**
Don.10/12/25-27/3/26.**G.**
Don.23/7-18/9/26.**H.**
Don.12-29/1/27.**H.**
Don.7/11/27-25/2/28.**G.**
Don.3-26/4/28.**L.**
Corridor tender put on.
Don.18/2-14/4/29.**G.**
Don.3-18/7/30.**G.**
Don.27/5-18/7/31.**G.**
Don.11/5-9/7/32.**G.**
Don.15/6-22/7/33.**G.**
Tender type change.
Don.8/6-19/7/34.**G.**
Don.10/9-31/10/35.**G.**
Don.27/11/36-14/1/37.**G.**
Don.25/1-25/2/38.**G.**
Don.19/5-8/7/39.**G.**
Don.8/1-8/2/41.**G.**

Repairs:- **C/H**-Casual Heavy.   **C/L**-Casual Light.   **G**-General.   **H**-Heavy.   **H/I**-Heavy Intermediate.   **L**-Light.   **L/I**-Light Intermediate.   **N/C**-Non-Classified.
Works:-   Cow - Cowlairs.   Dar - Darlington.   Don - Doncaster.   Gat - Gateshead.   Gor - Gorton.   Hay - Haymarket shed.   SRX - St Rollox.

Don.1-13/12/41.**L.**
Don.8/8-19/9/42.**G.**
Don.3/4-13/5/44.**G.**
Don.5-26/7/45.**G.**
Don.20/3/46- *Into shops for rebuilding to Class A3.*

BOILERS:
7765
7784 (new) 25/2/28
7694 (ex2548) 9/7/32
7793 (ex4476) 31/10/35
7796 (ex2570) 14/1/37
7789 (ex2548) 8/7/39

TENDERS:
5257 30/8/24-3/4/28
5327 26/4/28-2/5/28
5256 2/5/28-6/5/28
5327 6/5/28-15/6/33
5273 22/7/33-1/12/41
5566 13/12/41-

SHEDS:
Grantham
Kings Cross 11/3/27
Grantham 27/3/27
Kings Cross 26/4/28
Doncaster 31/10/35

2548
GALTEE MORE

DONCASTER 1604

To traffic 27/9/24

REPAIRS:
Gor.18-25/10/24.**L.**
Don.22-27/12/24.**L.**
Don.15/3-23/6/26.**G.**
Don.2/5-21/6/27.**G.**
Don.8/8-20/9/27.**H.**
Don.24/8-18/10/28.**G.**
Don.21/10-6/12/29.**G.**
Don.20/5-5/7/30.**G.**
Don.13/5-11/7/31.**G.**
Don.25/8-5/9/31.**L.**
Don.25/2-30/4/32.**G.**
Don.20/4-16/6/33.**G.**
Don.9/4-23/5/34.**G.**
Don.12/3-17/4/35.**G.**
Don.18/2-15/4/36.**G.**
Don.13/3-28/4/37.**G.**
Don.9/2-26/3/38.**G.**
Don.22/4/38.**L.**
Don.8/3-28/4/39.**G.**
Don.8/4-15/5/40.**G.**
Don.10/1-15/2/41.**L.**
Don.18/2-26/3/42.**G.**
Don.12-14/5/42.**L.**
Don.1-27/11/43.**G.**
Don.31/10-18/11/44.**L.**
Don.20/8/45- *Into shops for rebuilding to Class A3.*

BOILERS:
7766
7775 (ex2557) 5/7/30
7694 (ex4481) 11/7/31
7879 (ex2560) 30/4/32
7771 (ex2560) 17/4/35
7789 (ex2549) 26/3/38
7770 (ex2558) 28/4/39

TENDERS:
5258 27/9/24-30/9/31
5270 30/9/31-20/4/33
5269 16/6/33-8/4/34
5270 8/4/34-29/11/41
5262 6/12/41-

SHEDS:
Grantham
Doncaster 5/7/30
Grantham 17/8/30
New England 5/1/42
Grantham 10/7/42
New England 11/10/42
Grantham 8/5/43
Doncaster 13/10/43
Grantham 12/10/44
Doncaster 6/12/44

2549
PERSIMMON

DONCASTER 1605

To traffic 25/10/24

REPAIRS:
Don.16-19/3/25.**L.**
Don.1-4/7/25.**L.**
Don.3-17/10/25.**L.**
Don.7/1-17/4/26.**G.**
Don.27/5-23/7/27.**G.**
Don.30/8-27/10/28.**G.**
Don.22/1-1/3/29.**L.**
Don.5-24/4/29.**H.**
Don.7/4-31/5/30.**G.**
Don.7/1-21/3/31.**G.**
Don.11/1-27/2/32.**G.**
Don.5/12/32-25/1/33.**G.**
Don.8/5-2/6/33.**H.**
Don.20/4-13/6/34.**G.**
Don.13/4-25/5/35.**G.**
Don.5-21/6/35.**L.**
Don.20/4-28/5/36.**G.**
Don.10-21/8/36.**L.**
Don.8/4-13/5/37.**G.**
Don.3/2-19/3/38.**G.**
Don.20/4/38.**L.**
Don.18/2-25/3/39.**G.**
Don.19/4-25/5/40.**G.**
Don.12-19/8/40.**L.**
Don.23/9-14/10/40.**L.**
Don.30/1-19/3/42.**G.**
Don.30/5-10/6/42.**L.**
Don.16/11/43- *Into shops for rebuilding to Class A3.*

BOILERS:
7767
7777 (ex2559) 27/10/28
7790 (ex2571) 27/2/32
7789 (ex2543) 28/5/36
7698 (ex2559) 13/5/37

TENDERS:
5259 25/10/24-27/3/32
5264 27/3/32-20/4/34
5289 13/6/34-19/2/40
5259 28/2/40-

SHEDS:
Doncaster
Grantham 16/7/27
New England 5/1/42

Grantham 10/7/42
New England 11/10/42
Grantham 7/5/43

2550
BLINK BONNY

DONCASTER 1606

To traffic 12/11/24

REPAIRS:
Gor.13-20/12/24.**L.**
Don.16-23/7/25.**L.**
Don.19/6-28/8/26.**G.**
Don.1/9-8/11/27.**G.**
Don.17/12/28-25/1/29.**G.**
Don.9/1-1/3/30.**G.**
Don.9/1-21/3/31.**G.**
Don.29/1-19/3/32.**G.**
Don.10/3-3/5/33.**G.**
Don.9/4-25/5/34.**G.**
Don.26/3-16/5/35.**G.**
Don.31/3-20/5/36.**G.**
Don.5/4-8/5/37.**G.**
Don.21/3-5/5/38.**G.**
Don.20/4-27/5/39.**G.**
Don.23/4-1/6/40.**G.**
Don.30/1-14/3/42.**G.**
Don.9/12/43-18/1/44.**G.**
Don.15/9-7/10/44.**L.**
Don.17/9/45- *Into shops for rebuilding to Class A3.*

BOILERS:
7768
7696 (ex4475) 25/1/29
7774 (ex2556) 21/3/31
7778 (ex2545) 3/5/33
7703 (ex4477) 25/5/34
7696 (ex2582) 20/5/36
7765 (ex4477) 5/5/38

TENDERS:
5260 25/10/24-

SHEDS:
Gorton
Grantham 9/2/25
New England 5/1/42
Grantham 2/5/43
New England 11/6/44
Gorton 14/7/44
Kings Cross 29/10/44
Grantham 11/11/44

2551
PRINCE PALATINE

DONCASTER 1607

To traffic 29/11/24

REPAIRS:
Don.29/12/24-2/1/25.**L.**
Don.9-12/1/25.**L.**
Don.11-16/3/25.**L.**
Don.30/6-25/9/26.**G.**
Don.20/10/27-2/2/28.**G.**
Don.8/10-20/12/28.**G.**
Don.30/9-23/11/29.**G.**
Don.21/8-23/10/30.**G.**
Don.29/12/30-14/1/31.**L.**
Don.18/5-4/7/31.**H.**

Don.12/4-16/6/32.**H.**
Don.10/6-12/7/33.**G.**
Don.10/10-16/11/34.**G.**
Don.23/9-9/11/35.**G.**
Don.1/10-4/11/36.**G.**
Don.12-17/11/36.**N/C.**
Don.27/7-28/8/37.**G.**
Don.6/4-3/5/38.**L.**
Don.25/10-30/11/38.**G.**
Don.2/2-9/3/40.**G.**
Don.24/6/41- *Into shops for rebuilding to Class A3.*

BOILERS:
7769
7768 (ex2550) 23/11/29
7774 (ex2550) 12/7/33
7794 (ex2552) 4/11/36

TENDERS:
5261 29/11/24-24/6/41

SHEDS:
Gorton
Grantham 9/2/25

2552
SANSOVINO

DONCASTER 1608

To traffic 11/12/24

REPAIRS:
Don.18/6-21/8/26.**G.**
Don.3-12/3/27.**L.**
Don.11/11/27-25/2/28.**G.**
Don.7/3-4/5/29.**G.**
Don.16/8-6/9/29.**L.**
Don.27/3-6/6/30.**G.**
Don.21/11-20/12/30.**H.**
Don.30/7-24/9/31.**G.**
Don.15/10-9/12/32.**G.**
Don.3/11-15/12/33.**G.**
Dar.5-20/9/34.**N/C.**
Don.4/1-12/2/35.**G.**
Don.29/4-23/6/36.**G.**
Don.25/3-1/5/37.**G.**
Don.17/3-29/4/38.**G.**
Don.20/4-2/6/39.**G.**
Don.20/7-31/8/40.**G.**
Don.6-27/6/42.**H/I.**
Don.12/7/43- *Into shops for rebuilding to Class A3.*

BOILERS:
7770
7794 (ex2579) 24/9/31
7647 (ex4473) 23/6/36

TENDERS:
5262 29/11/24-7/6/28
5329 7/6/28-10/8/28
5228 10/8/28-7/3/29
5272 5/4/29-30/6/29
5265 30/6/29-16/8/29
5274 6/9/29-12/7/43

SHEDS:
Kings Cross
Neasden 14/6/39
Kings Cross 21/11/42
Copley Hill 15/2/43

2553
MANNA
PRINCE OF WALES from
11/11/26

DONCASTER   1609

To traffic 31/12/24

REPAIRS:
Don.12/7-2/10/26.**G.**
Don.9-18/12/26.**L.**
Don.26-28/1/27.**L.**
Don.17/1-11/5/28.**G.**
Don.6/11-21/12/29.**G.**
Don.19-27/5/30.**L.**
Don.10-28/6/30.**H.**
Don.9/4-30/5/31.**G.**
Don.28/8-5/9/31.**L.**
Don.18/7-23/9/32.**G.**
Don.29/11/33-19/1/34.**G.**
Don.4/6-18/7/35.**G.**
Don.21/7-1/9/36.**G.**
Don.17-28/12/36.**L.**
Don.15/9-15/10/37.**G.**
Don.21/2-4/3/38.**G.**
Don.2/5/38.*Weigh.*
Don.7/11-2/12/38.**L.**
Don.22/7-2/9/39.**G.**
Don.13/5-18/6/41.**G.**
Don.18/6/43- *Into shops for rebuilding to Class A3.*

BOILERS:
7771
7695 (ex4474) 21/12/29
7801 (ex2579) 23/9/32
7798 (ex2572) 18/7/35
7763 (ex2571) 1/9/36

TENDERS:
5263 31/12/24-21/7/36
5264 1/9/36-

SHEDS:
Gorton
Kings Cross 28/1/25
Doncaster 11/5/28
Copley Hill 28/10/36
Doncaster 27/2/40
Grantham 18/3/40
New England 11/10/42

2554
WOOLWINDER

DONCASTER   1610

To traffic 31/12/24

REPAIRS:
Don.19-30/1/25.**L.**
Don.5/2-13/3/25.**L.**
Don.4-21/1/26.**L.**
Don.19/11/26-29/1/27.**G.**
Don.12/10-3/11/27.**L.**
Don.12/3-8/6/28.**G.**
Don.31/5-16/7/29.**G.**
Don.25/4-14/6/30.**G.**
Don.27/4-20/6/31.**G.**
Don.3-31/12/31.**H.**
Don.23/5-22/7/32.**G.**

Don.7/9-25/10/33.**G.**
Don.17/10-24/11/34.**G.**
Don.1/10-15/11/35.**G.**
Don.25/4-6/6/36.**G.**
Don.2-14/12/36.**L.**
Don.2/4-8/5/37.**G.**
Don.12/3-23/4/38.**G.**
Don.30/12/38-16/2/39.**G.**
Gor.16-23/12/39.**L.**
Don.29/4-5/6/40.**G.**
Don.13/2-1/3/41.**L.**
After collision in Marylebone tunnel.
Don.23/4/42- *Into shops for rebuilding to Class A3.*

BOILERS:
7772
7771 (ex2553) 14/6/30
7780 (ex2561) 20/6/31
7792 (ex4473) 24/11/34
7803 (ex2569) 6/6/36

TENDERS:
5264 31/12/24-27/3/32
5258 27/3/32-23/4/42

SHEDS:
Doncaster
Grantham 29/4/27
Kings Cross 15/7/29
Grantham 6/10/29
Doncaster 10/10/29
Grantham 16/10/29
Gorton 18/8/39

2555
CENTENARY

DONCASTER   1611

To traffic 7/2/25

REPAIRS:
Don.25-27/3/25.**L.**
Don.13-16/7/25.**L.**
Don.30/12/26-25/3/27.**G.**
Valve gear modification.
Don.11-12/1/28.**L.**
Don.27-31/1/28.**L.**
Don.2/6-19/7/28.**G.**
Don.1/8-5/9/29.**G.**
Don.14/11/30-10/1/31.**G.**
Don.9-18/4/31.**L.**
Don.14/3-6/5/32.**G.**
Don.26/10-9/12/32.**H.**
Don.29/1-21/3/34.**G.**
Don.18/9-6/11/35.**G.**
Don.17/9-22/10/36.**G.**
Don.27/11-3/12/36.**N/C.**
Don.18/11-12/12/37.**G.**
Don.10/3-29/4/39.**G.**
Don.7/10-9/11/40.**G.**
Don.17/9-24/10/42.**G.**
Don.5/7/44- *Into shops for rebuilding to Class A3.*

BOILERS:
7773
7767 (ex2549) 5/9/29
7797 (ex2572) 6/5/32
7792 (ex2554) 22/10/36

TENDERS:
5265 31/1/25-2/6/28
5257 19/7/28-

SHEDS:
Doncaster
Gorton 9/2/25
Doncaster 24/2/25
Grantham 5/10/29
Doncaster 17/10/29
Grantham 13/12/35
New England 1/1/36
Kings Cross 5/2/36
New England 19/2/36
Grantham 23/10/36
Copley Hill 29/10/36
Doncaster 26/2/40
Grantham 18/3/40
Doncaster 11/12/41

2556
ORMONDE

DONCASTER   1612

To traffic 18/2/25

REPAIRS:
Don.2-14/11/25.**L.**
Don.20/11/26-2/2/27.**G.**
Don.3/2-26/5/28.**G.**
Don.8/5-21/6/29.**G.**
Don.10/12/29-31/1/30.**G.**
Don.12-19/3/30.**N/C.**
Don.17/9-6/11/30.**G.**
Don.24/9-2/11/31.**G.**
Don.7/4-4/6/32.**H.**
Don.20/12/32-21/2/33.**G.**
Don.4/1-17/2/34.**G.**
Don.10/1-15/2/35.**G.**
Don.28/6-10/7/35.**L.**
Don.8/1-22/2/36.**G.**
Don.19/10-3/12/36.**G.**
Don.16/11-22/12/37.**G.**
Don.11/5/38.**L.**
Don.5/12/38-19/1/39.**G.**
Cow.16-17/5/40.**L.**
Bogie springs.
Don.8/7-9/8/40.**G.**
Don.14/11-12/12/41.**G.**
Cow.21-31/12/42.**L.**
Don.29/6-13/8/43.**G.**
Don.4/5-21/6/45.**G.**
Don.28/11/46- *Into shops for rebuilding to Class A3.*

BOILERS:
7774
7776 (ex2559) 6/11/30
7768 (ex2551) 17/2/34
7777 (ex2558) 3/12/36

TENDERS:
5266 31/1/25-3/2/28
5329 26/5/28-7/6/28
5262 7/6/28-14/11/41
5273 12/12/41-

SHEDS:
Grantham
Kings Cross 1/6/28
Grantham 7/6/28

Doncaster 15/9/38
Haymarket 9/3/39
St Margarets 15/3/39
Eastfield 2/2/40
Haymarket 4/12/40
Dundee 7/3/43
Haymarket 24/4/43

RENUMBERED:
No.57. 8/9/46

2557
BLAIR ATHOL

DONCASTER   1613

To traffic 28/2/25

REPAIRS:
Don.17-23/3/25.**L.**
Don.27/10-31/12/26.**G.**
Don.17/1-8/5/28.**G.**
Don.22/10-3/11/28.**L.**
Don.22/3-11/5/29.**G.**
Don.2/12/29-11/1/30.**H.**
Don.19/3-15/5/30.**H.**
Don.19/3-4/5/31.**G.**
Don.11/4-21/5/32.**G.**
Don.28/4-21/6/33.**G.**
Don.23/5-14/7/34.**G.**
Don.30/4-14/6/35.**G.**
Don.3-4/7/35.
Tender repair only.
Don.10/6-18/7/36.**G.**
Don.20-27/8/36.**L.**
Don.5/5-17/6/37.**G.**
Don.27/4-8/6/38.**G.**
Don.25/5-15/7/39.**G.**
Don.1-31/7/40.**G.**
Don.20/3-23/4/42.**G.**
Don.16-26/6/43.**L.**
Don.7/3-13/4/44.**G.**
Don.24/10/45- *Into shops for rebuilding to Class A3.*

BOILERS:
7775
7773 (ex2555) 11/5/29
7769 (ex2559) 21/6/33
7786 (ex2575) 18/7/36
7767 (ex4471) 8/6/38
7799 (ex2562) 15/7/39

TENDERS:
5267 28/2/25-22/3/29
5269 11/5/29-28/4/33
5270 21/6/33-8/4/34
5269 8/4/34-27/4/38
5211 8/6/38-1/7/40
5279 31/7/40-18/8/41
5271 18/8/41-

SHEDS:
Gorton
Grantham 25/3/25
Kings Cross 21/11/42
Copley Hill 15/2/43
Doncaster 29/9/43

Repairs:- **C/H**-Casual Heavy.   **C/L**-Casual Light.   **G**-General.   **H**-Heavy.   **H/I**-Heavy Intermediate.   **L**-Light.   **L/I**-Light Intermediate.   **N/C**-Non-Classified.
Works:-   **Cow** - Cowlairs.   **Dar** - Darlington.   **Don** - Doncaster.   **Gat** - Gateshead.   **Gor** - Gorton.   **Hay** - Haymarket shed.   **SRX** - St Rollox.

In addition to their main-line duties, Pacifics could often be seen on race specials and 4474 is here passing mile post 55 near Cambridge, on its way to Newmarket.

1475 was the first to use the larger turntable at the resited Kings Cross Station loco yard, which became operational in the last week of 1923. Shedded new to Kings Cross, 1475 remained on the Top Shed allocation until June 1940.

4475 *FLYING FOX* was one of those selected for the non-stop running to and from Edinburgh and was coupled with a corridor tender from July 1928 until October 1936 when the tender was taken off to run with A4 class No.4482 *GOLDEN EAGLE*. Here, on the 9th June 1935, 4475 is at New England.

In 1935 no.4477 was still shuttling between Doncaster and London and seen here at Ganwick has one of the heavy expresses from Kings Cross. It has now been cut down to the Group Standard Loading Gauge of which 4477 very rarely had to take advantage.

New to traffic on the 16th June 1923 as L & N E R 1477, the 'N' suffix was added to the number when out from a light repair on 25th September 1923, and practically all its work as an A1 was done from Doncaster shed. Here it has the heavy 4 p.m. express from London.

Now nothing but nostalgia - a thrilling picture for enthusiasts, and clean steam to dispel any claims as to pollution. 4475 on a down fast in the mid-1930s.

1478 was the first of the 1923-built Pacifics to have the ampersand omitted, starting into traffic on the 30th June with L N E R on its tender. From a light repair on 26th September it came out with the 'N' suffix added to the number, as here at Wood Green in 1924 on a down express. It did not get its *HERMIT* nameplates until November 1925.

In March 1939 the Great Northern main line was so well provided for with A4 and V2 class locomotives that it was able to release seven A1s to work between Manchester (London Road) and London (Marylebone). 4478 was one of that batch and here is leaving Nottingham (Victoria) for Manchester.

4478 here in the summer of 1939 is at Northwood on the 3.20 p.m. from Marylebone to Manchester. It continued working on the G.C.main line until November 1942 when it returned to the G.N.line but running from Kings Cross instead of from Doncaster.

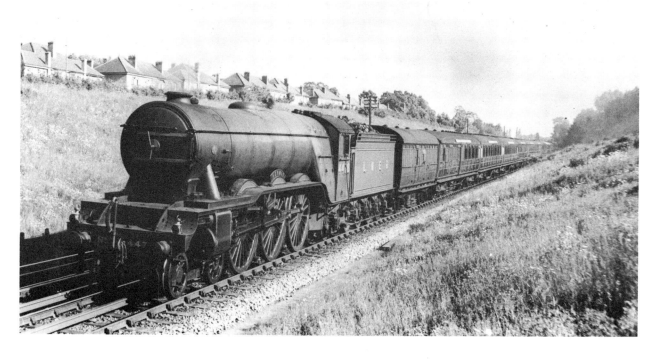

2558
TRACERY

DONCASTER   1614

To traffic 25/3/25

REPAIRS:
Don.30/8-13/11/26.**G.**
Don.18-21/1/27.**L.**
Don.17/10-23/12/27.**G.**
Don.27/2-15/3/28.**L.**
Don.31/8-17/11/28.**G.**
Diamond soot blower.
Don.27-28/5/29.**L.**
Don.5/9-19/10/29.**G.**
Don.31/10-20/12/30.**G.**
Don.26/3-16/4/31.**L.**
Don.18/9-6/11/31.**G.**
Don.9/6-23/7/32.**H.**
Don.30/6-14/8/33.**G.**
Don.25/4-16/6/34.**G.**
Don.15/5-21/6/35.**G.**
Don.23/6-1/8/36.**G.**
Don.22/5-26/6/37.**G.**
Don.26/4/38.**L.**
Don.2/6-9/7/38.**G.**
Don.13-19/9/38.**L.**
Speed recorder for G.C.line.
Don.16/9-11/11/39.**G.**
Don.5/11-11/12/40.**G.**
Don.20/6/42- *Into shops for rebuilding to Class A3.*

BOILERS:
7776
7701 (ex4480) 23/12/27
7698 (ex4477) 17/11/28
7777 (ex2549) 23/7/32
7770 (ex2574) 1/8/36
7696 (ex2550) 9/7/38
7772 (ex4472) 11/12/40

TENDERS:
5268 28/2/25-22/5/37
5645 26/6/37-5/11/40
5281 11/12/40-

SHEDS:
Gorton
Grantham 17/4/25
Gorton 19/9/38

2559
THE TETRARCH

DONCASTER   1615

To traffic 28/3/25

REPAIRS:
Don.3/1-21/3/27.**G.**
Don.15-22/8/27.**L.**
Don.5/1-21/4/28.**G.**
Don.15/3-2/5/29.**G.**
Don.22/4-7/6/30.**G.**
Don.3/9-22/10/31.**G.**
Don.7-8/6/32.**L.** *New tyres.*
Don.11/1-16/3/33.**G.**
Don.5/3-24/4/34.**G.**
Don.4/6-17/7/35.**G.**
Don.7/10-9/11/36.**G.**
Don.30/12/37-1/2/38.**G.**
Don.12/4/38.*Weigh.*

Don.22/11-31/12/38.**G.**
Don.26/1-2/3/40.**G.**
Don.31/8-18/9/40.**L.**
Don.2/12/40-17/1/41.**L.**
Don.25/11/41- *Into shops for rebuilding to Class A3.*

BOILERS:
7777
7776 (ex2558) 21/4/28
7769 /ex2551) 7/6/30
7698 (ex2558) 16/3/33
7769 (ex2557) 9/11/36

TENDERS:
5269 28/3/25-15/3/29
5253 2/5/29-13/11/36
5566 13/11/36-25/11/41

SHEDS:
Gorton
Kings Cross 28/4/25
Doncaster 30/4/27
Grantham 14/10/33
Doncaster 4/7/34
Grantham 9/3/38
Gateshead 9/3/39

2560
PRETTY POLLY

DONCASTER   1616

To traffic 17/4/25

REPAIRS:
Don.24/7-1/8/25.**L.**
Don.15/3-27/5/27.**G.**
Don.24/9-5/12/28.**G.**
Don.6/12/29-25/1/30.**G.**
Don.25/11/30-29/1/31.**G.**
Don.27/10-11/12/31.**G.**
Don.24/11/32-21/1/33.**G.**
Don.27/11/33-25/1/34.**G.**
Don.3/9-10/10/34.**G.**
Don.31/10-6/11/34.**L.**
Don.25-31/1/35.**L.**
Don.18/9-7/11/35.**G.**
Don.3-10/12/35.**N/C.**
Don.24/6-1/8/36.**G.**
Don.28/5-3/7/37.**G.**
Don.21/5-25/6/38.**G.**
Don.2/6-15/7/39.**G.**
Don.9-20/12/39.**L.**
Don.20/3-13/4/40.**L.**
Don.23/11-28/12/40.**G.**
Don.15/7-23/8/42.**G.**
Don.24/7-19/8/43.**L.**
Don.27/3/44- *Into shops for rebuilding to Class A3.*

BOILERS:
7778
7879 (ex4471) 29/1/31
7771 (ex2554) 11/12/31
7764 (ex2562) 10/10/34
7783 (ex2568) 25/6/38

TENDERS:
5270 28/3/25-30/9/31
5258 30/9/31-27/3/32
5229 27/3/32-28/5/37
5211 3/7/37-21/5/38
5290 25/6/38-

SHEDS:
Gorton
Kings Cross 23/5/25
Grantham 25/11/28
New England 10/10/42

2561
MINORU

DONCASTER   1617

To traffic 30/5/25

REPAIRS:
Don.9-14/11/25.**L.**
Don.30/11/26-5/2/27.**G.**
Don.11/5-11/7/28.**G.**
Don.3/10-30/11/29.**G.**
Don.2/1-3/3/31.**G.**
Don.18-22/5/31.**L.**
Don.24/2-9/4/32.**G.**
Don.9-10/6/32.**L.** *New tyres.*
Don.1/2-25/3/33.**G.**
Don.6/11-23/12/33.**G.**
Don.28/1-2/3/35.**G.**
Don.6/2-19/3/36.**G.**
Don.9/2-25/3/37.**G.**
Don.25/3-7/5/38.**G.**
Don.23-30/1/39.**L.**
Don.3/6-29/7/39.**G.**
Don.8/1-15/2/41.**G.**
Don.20/8-26/9/42.**H/I.**
Don.15/5/44- *Into shops for rebuilding to Class A3.*

BOILERS:
7780
7781 (ex2562) 3/3/31
7695 (ex2553) 25/3/33
7785 (ex2565) 25/3/37
7771 (ex2548) 7/5/38
7773 (ex2566) 15/2/41

TENDERS:
5271 30/5/25-11/5/28
5223 11/7/28-9/2/37
5477 25/3/37-25/3/38
5643 7/5/38-

SHEDS:
Gorton
Doncaster 20/6/25
Grantham 19/4/26
Kings Cross 27/3/27
New England 25/6/40

2562
ISINGLASS

DONCASTER   1618

To traffic 27/6/25 with 'E' type superheater.

REPAIRS:
Dar.8-9/12/25.**L.**
Raven F.S.A. fitted.
Gat.22/2-1/3/26.**L.**
Dar.9-18/3/26.**L.**
Don.28/9-24/12/26.**G.**
Don.21/11/27-10/3/28.**G.**
Diamond soot blower fitted.
Don.8/3-8/5/29.**G.**
Don.6/12/29-1/2/30.**H.**
Don.23/7-4/9/30.**G.** *'E' type superheater removed.*
Don.9/4-5/6/31.**G.**
Don.9/5-29/6/32.**G.**
Don.21/3-12/5/33.**G.**
Don.20/10-21/11/33.**L.**
Don.22/6-3/8/34.**G.**
Don.2/11-15/12/34.**H.**
Don.18/11-28/12/35.**G.**
Don.25/11/36-7/1/37.**G.**
Don.9-20/8/37.**L.**
Don.31/1-4/3/38.**G.**
Don.20/4/38.**L.**
Don.24/2-21/4/39.**G.**
Don.17/3-20/4/41.**G.**
Don.27/5-7/7/43.**G.**
Don.1-15/3/44.**L.**
Don.16/11-2/12/44.**H/I.**
Don.6/3/46- *Into shops for rebuilding to Class A3.*

BOILERS:
7781
7764 (ex2546) 4/9/30
7781 (ex2561) 12/5/33
7799 (ex2567) 7/1/37
7793 (ex2547) 4/3/38

TENDERS:
5272 27/6/25-8/3/29
5267 8/5/29-25/11/36
5277 7/1/37-31/1/38
5231 4/3/38-

SHEDS:
Doncaster
Gateshead 7/12/25
Doncaster 26/9/26
Grantham 14/10/28
King Cross 30/4/38
Leicester Cen. 24/8/39
Neasden 3/12/39
Gorton 23/2/41
Kings Cross 22/11/42
Gorton 9/7/44
Copley Hill 3/8/44
Doncaster 22/1/45

2563
WILLIAM WHITELAW
TAGALIE from 2/8/41

N.B.Loco.Co. 23101

To traffic 9/7/24

REPAIRS:
Cow.9-25/6/25.**L**. *Painted
for Centenary Procession.*
Cow.14/10-28/11/25.**L**.
Cow.6-8/4/26.**L**.
Cow.18/8-4/9/26.**L**.
Cow.8/11/26-18/2/27.**G**.
Cow.20/3-27/4/28.**L**.
Modified valve gear.
Cow.17/5/28.**L**.
Cow.10-18/1/29.**L**
Cow.3/4-31/5/29.**G**.
Variable F.S.A. fitted.
Cow.17-21/6/29.**L**.
Cow.20/1-8/2/30.**L**.
Cow.25/4-2/6/30.**L**.
Cow.16-17/6/30.**L**.
Cow.4-11/7/30.**L**.
Cow.29/7-1/8/30.**L**.
Cow.30/10-2/12/30.**G**.
Cow.2-12/2/31.**L**.
Cow.2-3/7/31.**L**.
Don.6/7-28/8/31.**G**.
Don.11/5-28/6/32.**G**.
Cow.19-29/8/32.**L**.
Don.9/3-27/4/33.**G**.
Don.16/1-3/3/34.**G**.
Don.6/12/34-19/1/35.**H**.
Don.6/6-19/7/35.**G**.
Don.27/8-10/10/36.**G**.
Don.2/9-9/10/37.**G**.
Don.17/3-29/4/39.**G**.
Cow.26/4-4/5/40.**L**.
Don.7/4-20/5/41.**G**.
Hudd A.T.C. fitted.
Don.21/7-2/8/41.**N/C**.
Change of name.
Don.1/10/42- *Into shops for
rebuilding to Class A3.*

BOILERS:
7785
7702 (ex4481) 31/5/29
7788 (ex2564) 27/4/33
7795 (ex4479) 20/5/41

TENDERS:
5273 9/7/24-16/5/28
5328 16/5/28-17/6/30
5479 17/6/30-10/7/30
5330 10/7/30-5/4/35
5584 5/4/35-

SHEDS:
Haymarket
Aberdeen 27/4/35
Eastfield 27/11/37
St Margarets 19/7/38
Dundee 12/1/40
Eastfield 11/10/40
Haymarket 4/12/40

2564
*KNIGHT OF THE
THISTLE
KNIGHT OF THISTLE
from 28/12/32*

N.B.Loco.Co. 23102

To traffic 14/7/24

REPAIRS:
Cow.11-29/8/25.**L**.
Cow.5/1-25/2/26.**G**.
Cow.25/2-6/5/27.**G**.
Cow.27-29/9/27.**L**.
Cow.1/5-19/6/28.**G**.
Modified valve gear.
Cow.25-26/2/29.**L**.
Cow.11/6-10/7/29.**G**.
Variable F.S.A. fitted.
Cow.4-14/12/29.**L**.
Cow.6/8-11/9/30.**L**.
Cow.5/1-18/2/31.**G**.
Cow.22/4-16/5/31.**L**.
Don.11/9-2/11/31.**G**.
Don.20-29/7/32.**L**.
Don.9/11/32-2/1/33.**G**.
Don.19/10-30/11/33.**G**.
Cow.14-23/8/34.**L**.
Don.21/11/34-8/1/35.**G**.
Don.12/2-3/4/36.**G**.
Don.18/5-25/6/37.**H**.
Don.29/10-25/11/37.**G**.
Cow.20-28/4/38.**L**.
Don.30/5-5/8/39.**G**.
Hudd A.T.C. fitted.
Cow.5-9/1/40.**L**.
Cow.23-25/5/40.**L**.
Don.1/5-7/6/41.**G**.
Don.6/6-8/7/42.**H/I**.
Don.27/1-4/3/44.**G**.
Don.5/11-20/12/45.**G**.
Don.12/2/47- *Into shops for
rebuilding to Class A3.*

BOILERS:
7786
7788 (ex2566) 10/7/29
7800 (ex2575) 2/1/33
7781 (ex2562) 25/11/37

TENDERS:
5274 14/7/24-2/7/28
5325 2/7/28-17/10/35
5581 17/10/35-18/5/37
5268 25/6/37-6/6/42
5283 8/7/42-23/1/44
5276 23/1/44-

SHEDS:
Haymarket
Eastfield 15/2/37
Carlisle 20/11/40
Haymarket 1/12/41

RENUMBERED:
No.65. 20/10/46

2565
MERRY HAMPTON

N.B.Loco.Co. 23103

To traffic 16/7/24

REPAIRS:
Cow.7/12/25-21/1/26.**G**.
Named.
Dar.8/6-15/9/26.**L**.
*Cramlington derailment. Also
had the legend CLASS 4.6.2.
applied to buffer beam at
same shopping.*
Cow.20-27/9/26.**L**.
Cow.20/10-5/11/26.**L**.
Cow.16-19/8/27.**L**.
Cow.17/1-4/4/28.**G**.
Modified valve gear.
Cow.8/1-20/3/29.**G**.
Cow.25/7-10/8/29.**L**.
Variable F.S.A. fitted.
Cow.14/4-25/6/30.**G**.
Cow.7-10/7/30.**L**.
Tablet apparatus fitted.
Cow.4-22/12/30.**L**.
Cow.25/2-3/3/31.**L**.
Cow.15/5-12/6/31.**L**.
Cow.24-25/6/31.**L**.
Don.29/1-12/4/32.**G**.
Don.29/9-15/11/32.**H**.
Broken frame.
Don.2/3-19/4/34.**G**.
Don.25/12/34-27/1/35.**H**.
Cow.13-14/11/35.**L**.
Don.16/11/35-9/1/36.**G**.
Don.28/12/36-13/2/37.**G**.
Cow.4-8/5/37.**N/C**.
Don.13/4-23/5/38.**G**.
Don.13/3-6/4/39.**L**.
Don.29/1-9/3/40.**G**.
Hudd A.T.C. fitted.
Don.27/10-14/12/41.**G**.
Don.31/8-13/10/43.**G**.
Don.24-26/12/44.**L**.
Don.19/10/45- *Into shops for
rebuilding to Class A3.*

BOILERS:
7787
7785 (ex2566) 12/4/32
7797 (ex2555) 13/2/37

TENDERS:
5275 16/7/24-20/3/29
5330 20/3/29-4/7/29
5276 4/7/29-23/1/44
5283 23/1/44-19/10/45

SHEDS:
Haymarket
Gateshead 5/5/28
Haymarket 5/7/28
Dundee 6/10/30
Haymarket 17/8/31
Dundee 1/12/31
Aberdeen 10/8/35
Eastfield 4/5/36
Aberdeen 9/6/36
Eastfield 28/3/37
Carlisle 19/11/40
Haymarket 12/2/41

2566
LADAS

N.B.Loco.Co. 23104

To traffic 14/8/24

REPAIRS:
Gat.27/2-16/3/25.**L**.
Cow.3-25/5/26.**G**.
Cow.5-13/8/26.**L**.
Cow.17/5-13/7/27.**G**.
Dar.3/8-6/9/27.**L**.
Cow.22/2-6/3/28.**L**.
Cow.5/6-13/7/28.**G**.
Cow.6-13/9/28.**L**.
Cow.25/4-19/6/29.**G**.
Variable F.S.A. fitted.
Cow.26/6-1/7/29.**L**.
Cow.9-27/11/29.**L**.
Cow.6-10/7/30.**G**.
Tablet apparatus fitted.
Cow.26/3-28/4/31.**L**.
Don.12/11/31-12/1/32.**G**.
Don.27/1-24/3/33.**G**.
Don.24/11/33-18/1/34.**G**.
Don.29/11/34-10/1/35.**G**.
Cow.26/6-4/7/35.**L**. *Flaman
Speed Recorder attached.*
Cow.22-23/10/35.**L**.
Cow.29/10-1/11/35.**L**.
Don.21/1-28/2/36.**G**.
Don.19/12/36-5/2/37.**G**.
Don.9/6-9/7/38.**G**.
Don.23-25/8/38.**L**.
Dar.21-28/7/39.**L**.
Left leading hot-box.
Don.20/9/39- *Into shops for
rebuilding to Class A3.*

BOILERS:
7788
7785 (ex2563) 19/6/29
7789 (ex2567) 12/1/32
7767 (ex2555) 24/3/33
7773 (ex2557) 18/1/34

TENDERS:
5276 14/8/24-4/7/29
5330 4/7/29-10/7/30
5479 10/7/30-

SHEDS:
Haymarket
Dundee 18/8/30
Eastfield 7/2/37

2567
SIR VISTO

N.B.Loco.Co. 23105

To traffic 14/8/24

REPAIRS:
*Cow.?/10/27-?/2/28.**G**.
Cow.?/12/28-23/2/29.**L**.
Cow.19/10/29-?/12/29.**G**.
Cow.25-28/6/30.**N/C**.
Tablet apparatus fitted.*

Repairs:- **C/H**-Casual Heavy. **C/L**-Casual Light. **G**-General. **H**-Heavy. **H/I**-Heavy Intermediate. **L**-Light. **L/I**-Light Intermediate. **N/C**-Non-Classified.
Works:- Cow - Cowlairs. Dar - Darlington. Don - Doncaster. Gat - Gateshead. Gor - Gorton. Hay - Haymarket shed. SRX - St Rollox.

The next twenty were built by North British Locomotive Co. Glasgow, and here in their Hyde Park Works the one suspended from the crane (and already painted) emerged on the 9th July 1924, with *WILLIAM WHITELAW* nameplates. The other Pacific, being given its first steaming, duly went into traffic as No.2568, but ran without name until October 1925.

The above shopping dates, although not complete for the period from August 1924 until February 1931, are compiled from observations made at Cowlairs Works and are therefore only representative. The reason why a true record cannot be given is because the 'Engine History Card' for this locomotive was in fact lost during the re-organisation of the Regions shortly after Nationalisation when Carlisle Canal shed became part of the London Midland Region. Those listed below are a true record of events.

Don.26/2-29/4/31.**G.**
Don.30/11/31-26/1/32.**H.**
Don.13/10-24/11/32.**G.**
Don.4/12/33-27/1/34.**G.**
Don.15/4-1/6/35.**G.**
Don.17/11-24/12/36.**G.**
Don.30/5-30/6/38.**G.**
Don.26/5-15/7/39.**G.**
Hudd A.T.C. fitted.
Cow.25-27/4/40.**L.**
Don.6/3-11/4/41.**G.**
Cow.8-12/8/41.**L.**
Don.26/3-2/4/43.**H.**
Don.10/3-14/4/45.**G.**
Don.31/1-20/3/47.**G.**
Don.3/11/48- *Into shops for rebuilding to Class A3.*

BOILERS:
7789
7786 (ex2564) ?/12/29
7799 (ex2568) 26/1/32
7798 (ex2553) 24/12/36

TENDERS:
5277 14/8/24-17/11/36
5637 24/12/36-

SHEDS:
Haymarket
Dundee 18/8/30, *the loco was here by 3/7/30 but 18/8/30 is the official date of transfer*
Eastfield 7/2/37
St Margarets 20/11/38
Eastfield 2/2/40
Carlisle 20/11/40

RENUMBERED:
No.68. 25/8/46
No.60068. 19/9/48

2568
SCEPTRE

N.B.Loco.Co.   23106

To traffic 19/9/24

REPAIRS:
Dar.9/11/25-12/2/26.**G.**
Dar.15-24/2/26.**L.**
Dar.15/12/26-7/1/27.**L.**

Dar.8/9-9/12/27.**G.**
Dar.23/12/27-6/1/28.**L.**
Dar.2/1-21/3/29.**G.**
'Joco' regulator valve. Flaman speed recorder fitted.
Dar.16-22/8/29.**N/C.**
Dar.22/1-14/3/30.**G.**
Gat.23/2-13/3/31.**L.**
Don.25/4-3/6/31.**G.**
Don.10/12/31-15/1/32.**H.**
Don.5/10-19/11/32.**G.**
Don.25/10-2/12/33.**G.**
Don.2/1-2/2/35.**G.**
Don.8/1-15/2/36.**G.**
Don.30/10-9/12/36.**G.**
Don.13/1-12/2/38.**G.**
Don.2-6/8/38.**L.**
Don.19-31/8/38.**L.**
Don.2/5-10/6/39.**G.**
Don.4-27/7/40.**G.**
Don.2/5/42- *Into shops for rebuilding to Class A3.*

BOILERS:
7790
7801 (ex2579) 21/3/29
7799 (ex2582) 14/3/30
7802 (ex2575) 3/6/31
7783 (ex2543) 2/12/33
7878 (ex4475) 12/2/38

TENDERS:
5278 19/9/24-7/5/40
5279 9/5/40-2/7/40
5211 27/7/40-2/5/42

SHEDS:
Gateshead
York 11/12/36

2569
GLADIATEUR

N.B.Loco.Co.   23107

To traffic 24/9/24

REPAIRS:
Gat.6/1-27/3/25.**L.**
Don.28/9-10/10/25.**L.**
Dar.22/3-10/8/26.**G.**
Dar.11-25/8/26.**L.**
Dar.23/9-14/10/26.**L.**
Dar.8-17/6/27.**L.**
Dar.29/12/27-22/3/28.**G.**
Dar.6-8/6/28.**N/C.**
Dar.3/12/28-27/2/29.**G.**
Dar.21/11/29-24/1/30.**G.**
Don.2/7-30/8/30.**G.**
Gat.14-29/1/31.**L.**
Don.9/11-14/12/31.**G.**
Don.4/1-15/2/33.**G.**
Don.27/9-9/11/33.**G.**
Don.5/10-10/11/34.**G.**
Dar.15/2-20/4/35.**L.**
Big end broken and motions damaged.
Don.10/2-31/3/36.**G.**
Dar.22-26/6/36.**N/C.**
Right Trailing Box heating.
Don.30/1-11/3/37.**G.**

Don.2/12/37-5/1/38.**G.**
Don.6/5/38.**L.**
Bogie changed.
Don.13/1-18/2/39.**G.**
Don.17/2-21/3/40.**G.**
Don.10/4-3/5/41.**G.**
Don.19-23/5/41.**L.**
Don.13/2-6/3/43.**G.**
Don.11-16/3/43.**N/C.**
Don.14/11-30/12/44.**G.**
Don.6-13/7/46.**L.**
Don.10/12/46- *Into shops for rebuilding to Class A3.*

BOILERS:
7791
7803 (ex2581) 27/2/29
7796 (ex2572) 24/1/30
7803 (ex2582) 14/12/31
7801 (ex2553) 31/3/36
7775 (ex2577) 3/5/41

TENDERS:
5279 24/9/24-24/4/28
5328 24/4/28-16/5/28
5273 16/5/28-6/6/28
5279 8/6/28-27/1/37
5285 11/3/37-8/2/43
5569 2/3/43-6/1/45
5477 6/1/45-

SHEDS:
Gateshead
York 18/4/38
Gateshead 6/5/46

RENUMBERED:
No.538. 17/3/46
No.70. 2/6/46

2570
TRANQUIL

N.B.Loco.Co.   23108

To traffic 27/9/24

REPAIRS:
Gat.17/4-11/5/25.**L.**
Dar.3/11/25-22/1/26.**G.**
Gat.10-11/3/26.**L.**
Dar.1/10-20/12/27.**G.**
Dar.15/2-26/4/29.**G.**
Dar.23/9/29.**N/C.**
Dar.16/12/29-12/2/30.**G.**
Gat.11-23/3/31.**L.**
Valves re-set.
Don.11/5-16/6/31.**G.**
Don.29/6-6/8/32.**G.**
Gat.25/10-7/11/32.**L.**
Valves re-set.
Dar.31/1-4/2/33.**L.**
Don.6/9-19/10/33.**G.**
Don.12/10-17/11/34.**G.**
Don.22/3-6/4/35.**L.**
Don.3/10-16/11/35.**G.**
Dar.21/4/36.*Weigh.*
Don.18/9-24/10/36.**G.**
Don.17/2-26/3/38.**G.**
Don.23/5-1/7/39.**G.**
Don.15/3-12/4/41.**G.**

Don.21/12/42-16/1/43.**G.**
Don.6/9/44- *Into shops for rebuilding to Class A3.*

BOILERS:
7792
7794 (ex2572) 26/4/29
7798 (ex2575) 12/2/30
7775 (ex2548) 16/6/31
7778 (ex2550) 17/11/34
7796 (ex2581) 16/11/35
7790 (ex2549) 24/10/36
7802 (ex2394) 26/3/38

TENDERS:
5280 27/9/24-20/3/35
5272 6/4/35-18/12/42
5291 17/1/43-

SHEDS:
Gateshead
York 11/11/36

2571
SUNSTAR

N.B.Loco.Co.   23109

To traffic 30/9/24

REPAIRS:
Dar.4/1-14/4/26.**G.**
Dar.3-11/6/26.**L.**
Dar.28/10-30/11/26.
Tender only.
Gat.7-9/3/27.**L.**
Dar.7/12/27-9/3/28.**G.**
Dar.4-12/6/28.**N/C.**
Dar.20/3-12/6/29.**G.**
Dar.28/10-28/11/29.**L.**
Don.10/3-10/4/30.**G.**
Dar.3-17/7/31.**N/C.**
Don.15/10-18/11/31.**G.**
Don.24/11/32-7/1/33.**G.**
Don.2/8-7/9/33.**G.**
Don.28/6-22/8/34.**G.**
Don.17/5-28/6/35.**G.**
Don.2/4-16/5/36.**G.**
Don.29/12/36-2/2/37.**G.**
Dar.16/2/37.*Weigh.*
Don.25/11-19/12/37.**G.**
Don.17/11-24/12/38.**G.**
Don.18/1-24/2/40.**G.**
Don.9-15/8/40.**L.**
R.H. frame straightened.
Don.10/6/41- *Into shops for rebuilding to Class A3.*

BOILERS:
7793
7790 (ex2568) 12/6/29
7763 (ex2545) 18/11/31
7787 (ex2576) 16/5/36

TENDERS:
5281 30/9/24-14/10/40
5476 14/10/40-

SHEDS:
Gateshead

Repairs:- **C/H**-Casual Heavy. **C/L**-Casual Light. **G**-General. **H**-Heavy. **H/I**-Heavy Intermediate. **L**-Light. **L/I**-Light Intermediate. **N/C**-Non-Classified.
Works:- Cow - Cowlairs. Dar - Darlington. Don - Doncaster. Gat - Gateshead. Gor - Gorton. Hay - Haymarket shed. SRX - St Rollox.

2572
ST GATIEN

N.B.Loco.Co.   23110

To traffic 3/10/24

REPAIRS:
Dar.17/3-15/4/25.
Tender only.
Dar.25/1-26/4/26.**G.**
Dar.25/5-1/6/26.**L.**
Dar.17/10-31/12/27.**G.**
Gat.26/10-16/11/28.**L.**
Gat.26-28/11/28.**L.**
Dar.28/11/28-8/2/29.**G.**
Dar.5-25/9/29.**H.**
Dar.27/9-18/12/29.**G.**
Dar.8-16/7/30.**N/C.**
Don.22/7-5/9/30.**G.**
Gat.27/8-9/9/31.**L.**
Don.24/11-24/12/31.**G.**
Don.25/8-8/10/32.**G.**
Dar.16-19/6/33.**N/C.**
Don.17/10-22/11/34.**G.**
Don.4/11-14/12/35.**G.**
Dar.4/5/36.*Weigh.*
Don.27/10-3/12/36.**G.**
Don.27/8-2/10/37.**G.**
Don.17/5/38.**L.**
Don.3/10-9/11/38.**G.**
Don.24/11-30/12/39.**G.**
Don.17/9-10/10/40.**L.**
Don.10/4-17/5/41.**G.**
Don.9-14/2/42.**L.**
Don.15/9-10/10/42.**G.**
Don.22/2-1/4/44.**G.**
Don.15/9/45- *Into shops for rebuilding to Class A3.*

BOILERS:
7794
7796 (ex2574) 8/2/29
7797 (ex2574) 18/12/29
7798 (ex2570) 24/12/31
7693 (ex4481) 22/11/34
7764 (ex2560) 30/12/39

TENDERS:
5282 3/10/24-26/10/36
5636 3/12/36-25/8/37
5292 2/10/37-31/8/42
5212 10/10/42-

SHEDS:
Gateshead
York 28/3/43

2573
HARVESTER

N.B.Loco.Co.   23111

To traffic 8/10/24

REPAIRS:
Dar.28/8-5/11/25.**L.**
Gat.30-31/3/26.**L.**
Dar.3-17/9/26.**G.**
Dar.22-30/9/26.**L.**
Dar.24/1-21/3/27.**L.**
New Right Hand cylirder.
Dar.10-23/6/27.**L.**
Dar.28/6-2/7/27.**L.**

Dar.31/1/28- *Into shops for rebuilding to Class A3.*

BOILERS:
7795

TENDERS:
5283 8/10/24-

SHEDS:
Gateshead

2574
ST FRUSQUIN

N.B.Loco.Co.   23112

To traffic 11/10/24

REPAIRS:
Gat.2-15/12/24.**L.**
Dar.20/4-28/5/25.**L.**
Dar.11-25/9/25.**L.**
Dar.8/10-3/11/25.**L.**
Dar.18-29/1/26.**L.**
Dar.9/11/26-8/1/27.**G.**
Dar.1-12/10/27.**L.**
Dar.11/10-14/12/28.**G.**
Dar.7-23/1/29.**N/C.**
Dar.30/1-8/2/29.**N/C.**

Gat.26/2-1/3/29.**L.**
Gat.7-17/5/29.**L.**
Valves re-set.
Dar.30/8-5/12/29.**G.**
Dar.14-18/7/30.**N/C.**
Don.7/10-18/11/30.**G.**
Don.17/12/31-27/1/32.**G.**
Gat.18-22/4/32.**L.**
Don.21/4-29/5/33.**G.**
Dar.5/10/33.**N/C.**
Don.13/3-28/4/34.**G.**
Don.28/2-30/3/35.**G.**
Don.17/3-29/4/36.**G.**
Don.19/3-8/5/37.**G.**
Don.22/3-30/4/38.**G.**
Don.8/7-19/8/39.**G.**
Don.28/12/40-30/1/41.**G.**
Don.1/6/42- *Into shops for rebuilding to Class A3.*

BOILERS:
7796
7797 (ex2575) 14/12/28
7792 (ex2570) 5/12/29
7770 (ex2552) 27/1/32
7778 (ex2570) 29/4/36

TENDERS:
5284 11/10/24-

SHEDS:
Gateshead

2575
GALOPIN

N.B.Loco.Co.   23113

To traffic 14/10/24

REPAIRS:
Dar.3/6-14/7/25.**L.**
Dar.3/8-7/10/25.**L.**
Dar.13/6-14/12/26.**G.**
Dar.31/5-15/6/27.**L.**
Dar.30/3-27/6/28.**G.**
Variable blast pipe fitted.
Gat.28/11-14/12/28.**L.**
Dar.10/1-20/2/29.**H.**
Dar.17/9-21/11/29.**G.**
Don.11/3-26/4/30.**G.**
Don.12/11-22/12/30.**G.**
Don.28/4-18/6/32.**G.**
Gat.11-20/10/32.**L.**
Valves re-set.
Don.12/6-21/7/33.**G.**
Don.19/4-31/5/34.**G.**
Don.18/2-20/3/35.**G.**
Dar.13-30/8/35.**L.**
Right Trailiing box heating.

Don.2/3-23/4/36.**G.**
Don.30/1-4/3/37.**G.**
Don.28/10-2/12/37.**G.**
Don.18/10-19/11/38.**G.**
Don.25/11-12/12/39.**G.**
Don.9/5/41- *Into shops for rebuilding to Class A3.*

BOILERS:
7797
7798 (ex2576) 27/6/28
7802 (ex2577) 21/11/29
7800 (ex2579) 22/12/30
7786 (ex2567) 18/6/32
7694 (ex2547) 23/4/36

TENDERS:
5285 14/10/24-27/1/37
5227 4/3/37-

SHEDS:
Gateshead

2576
THE WHITE KNIGHT

N.B.Loco.Co.   23114

To traffic 19/10/24

REPAIRS:
Dar.6/7-24/8/25.**L.**
Dar.26/8-23/9/25.**L.**
Dar.12/4-31/8/26.**G.**
Dar.14-27/9/26.**L.**
Dar.19-26/5/27.**L.**
Dar.22/6-1/7/27.**L.**
Gat.4-8/10/27.**L.**
Dar.20/4-15/6/28.**G.**
Dar.5-12/10/28.**N/C.**
Dar.3/5-30/8/29.**G.**
A.C.F.I. fitted.
Dar.7-25/2/30.**L.**
Don.8/5-14/6/30.**G.**
Don.8/1-2/3/31.**G.**
Gat.11-28/8/31.**L.**
Dar.3-11/12/31.**N/C.**
Dar.18/12/31-15/1/32.**N/C.**
Don.3/6-19/7/32.**G.**
Gat.9-18/11/32.**L.**
Valves re-set.
Don.7/6-14/7/33.**G.**
Dar.9-12/4/34.**L.**
Alteration to A.C.F.I. pump.
Don.31/5-7/7/34.**G.**
Don.5/9-25/10/35.**G.**
Don.25/9-30/10/36.**G.**
Don.14/9-16/10/37.**G.**
Don.5-19/1/38.**L.**
Don.4/5/38.**L.**
Don.4/11-9/12/38.**G.**
A.C.F.I. removed.
Don.16/1-16/2/40.**G.**
Don.24/5-5/7/41.**G.**
Don.23/5-5/6/42.**G.**
Don.31/5/43- *Into shops for rebuilding to Class A3.*

BOILERS:
7798
7795 (ex2573) 15/6/28
7787 (ex2565) 19/7/32
7879 (ex2548) 25/10/35
7780 (ex2581) 16/2/40

TENDERS:
5286 19/10/24-23/9/36
5482 30/10/36-27/5/43

SHEDS:
Gateshead
York 17/11/36
Gateshead 11/12/36
York 28/3/43

2577
NIGHT HAWK

N.B.Loco.Co.   23115

To traffic 24/10/24

REPAIRS:
Dar.5/3-5/8/26.**G.**
Dar.10-18/8/26.**L.**
Dar.8-23/9/26.**L.**
Gat.2-4/3/27.**L.**
Gat.25-27/4/27.**L.**
Gat.30/5-7/6/27.**L.**
Gat.28/6-4/7/27.**L.**
Dar.11/2-27/4/28.**G.**
Dar.4-10/5/28.**N/C.**
Dar.3/6-10/8/29.**G.**
Dar.15/10-19/12/29.**L.**

2547 in July 1939 had this official photograph taken because it had been fitted with four 3″ steel 'arch tubes' in the firebox to add heating surface and to promote water circulation. There was no external evidence of them, and only this one application was done. The extra tubes were removed in January 1941.

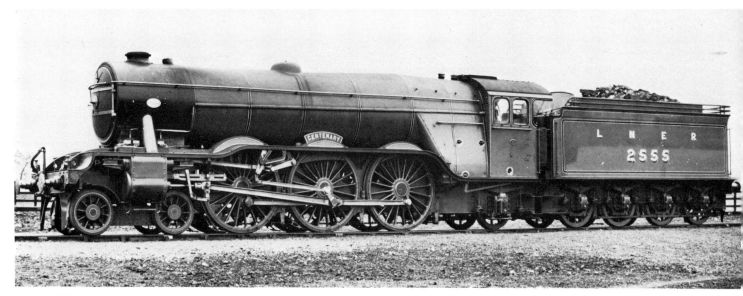

2555's 'official' was to show the fitting of nameplates, which were of the short variety.

2558's photograph arose from its being fitted 17th November 1928 with roller bearings in its motion.

Dar.21/5-6/6/30.**N/C.**
Don.16/10-26/11/30.**G.**
Don.29/12/31-16/1/32.**G.**
Dar.22/9-3/10/32.**N/C.**
Don.23/2-22/4/33.**G.**
Don.21/2-11/4/34.**G.**
Dar.2-4/8/34.**N/C.**
Dar.6-17/8/34.**N/C.**
Don.21/2-21/3/35.**G.**
Don.3/2-13/3/36.**G.**
Don.26/11-31/12/36.**G.**
84,969 miles.
Don.17/1-19/2/38.**G.**
Dar.8-29/8/38.**N/C.**
After derailment.
Don.10/3-22/4/39.**G.**
Don.17/1-1/2/40.**L.**
Don.21/6-20/7/40.**G.**
Don.24/1-28/2/42.**G.**
Don.17-22/4/42.**L.**
Don.9/12/43- *Into shops for rebuilding to Class A3.*

BOILERS:
7799
7802 (ex2580) 27/4/28
7793 (ex2571) 10/8/29
7766 (ex2548) 26/11/30
7775 (ex2570) 21/3/35
7796 (ex2547) 20/7/40

TENDERS:
5287 24/10/24-

SHEDS:
Gateshead
York 7/1/37

2578
BAYARDO

N.B.Loco.Co.   23116

To traffic 29/10/24

REPAIRS:
Gat.28-30/10/25.**L.**
For naming.
Dar.23/4-29/9/26.**G.**
Dar.30/3-15/7/27.**L.**
Dar.9/8-9/9/27.**L.**
Dar.21/2/28- *Into shops for rebuilding to Class A3.*

BOILERS:
7800

TENDERS:
5288 29/10/24-

SHEDS:
Heaton

2579
DICK TURPIN

N.B.Loco.Co.   23117

To traffic 3/11/24

REPAIRS:
Gat.23-27/10/25.**L.**
For naming.
Gat.15-29/3/26.**L.**
Dar.10/8-15/12/26.**G.**
Dar.14/1-2/2/27.**N/C.**
Dar.4/10-23/11/27.**L.**
Dar.27/1-6/2/28.**N/C.**
Dar.4-14/4/28.**N/C.**
Dar.26/10/28-16/1/29.**G.**
Dar.30/10-4/12/29.**L.**
Dar.11/1-3/3/30.**G.**
Don.17/3-23/4/31.**G.**
Dar.6-20/10/31.**N/C.**
Don.17/2-24/3/32.**G.**
Don.2/3-13/4/33.**G.**
Don.25/4-8/6/34.**G.**
Don.28-31/8/34.**L.**
Don.10/1-14/2/35.**G.**
Don.23/9-14/11/35.**G.**
Dar.21/11/35.*Weigh.*
Don.7/1-13/2/37.**G.**
Don.16/3-22/4/38.**G.**
Don.5/6-22/7/39.**G.**
Don.14/1-20/2/41.**G.**
Don.21/10/42- *Into shops for rebuilding to Class A3.*

BOILERS:
7801
7800 (ex2578) 16/1/29

7794 (ex2570) 3/3/30
7801 (exSpare) 23/4/31
7697 (ex4479) 24/3/32
7784 (exSpare) 8/6/34
7800 (ex2564) 22/4/38
7768 (ex4475) 20/2/41

TENDERS:
5289 3/11/24-20/4/34
5264 8/6/34-25/7/36
5263 26/7/36-12/3/38
5288 22/4/38-

SHEDS:
Heaton

Noted with Indicator shelter 4/1/27, with engine painted dull black and tender dull green. No L N E R on tender but 2579.

2580
SHOTOVER

N.B.Loco.Co.   23118

To traffic 9/11/24

REPAIRS:
Dar.24/11-1/12/24.**L.**
Gat.21-22/10/25.**L.**
For naming.

2558 ran from 26th June 1937 until 5th November 1940 coupled with a high-sided tender of the non-corridor variety with built-up front end as designed for the streamlined A4 class. Here in 1937 it is traversing the water troughs at Langley near Stevenage.

2559 had an American valve spindle guide put on when ex works 22nd October 1931.

Gat.29/3-9/4/26.**L.**
Gat.29/6-23/7/26.**L.**
Dar.14/9/26-19/1/27.**G.**
Dar.12/11/27- *Into shops for rebuilding to Class A3.*

BOILERS:
7802

TENDERS:
5290 9/11/24-

SHEDS:
Heaton

2581
NEIL GOW

N.B.Loco.Co.   23119

To traffic 30/11/24

REPAIRS:
Gat.6-11/11/25.**L.**
For naming.
Dar.5/10/26-8/2/27.**G.**

Dar.26/5-12/7/27.**L.**
Dar.9-11/1/28.**L.**
Dar.11/10/28-4/1/29.**G.**
Dar.27/5-16/7/29.**L.**
Dar.12-14/12/29.**L.**
Don.3/2-5/3/30.**G.**
Don.24/7-8/8/31.**G.**
Don.8/3-7/5/32.**G.**
Dar.23/11-23/12/32.**L.**
Dar.31/1-23/2/33.**H.**
New tyres.
Don.27/4-17/6/33.**G.**
Dar.30/6-14/7/33.**N/C.**
Don.12/5-20/6/34.**G.**
Dar.10-29/5/35.**L.**
Don.1/6-6/7/35.**G.**
Don.18/5-26/6/36.**G.**
Don.28/5-1/7/37.**G.**
Don.21/5-18/6/38.**G.**
Don.14/9-12/10/39.**G.**
Don.3-16/2/40.**L.**
Don.8-22/4/41.**G.**
Don.15/12/42- *Into shops for rebuilding to Class A3.*

BOILERS:

7803
7804 (ex2582) 4/1/29
7796 (ex2569) 7/5/32
7780 (ex2554) 6/7/35
7786 (ex2557) 18/6/38

TENDERS:
5291 30/11/24-7/12/42

SHEDS:
Heaton

2582
SIR HUGO

N.B.Loco.Co.   23120

To traffic 6/12/24

REPAIRS:
Dar.6-12/1/25.**L.**
Gat.17-19/11/25.**L.**
For naming.
Dar.11/1-30/6/27.**G.**
Gat.26/1-1/2/28.**L.**
Valves re-set.
Dar.18/4-20/6/28.**H.**
Gat.26-29/11/28.**L.**
Valves re-set.
Dar.10/1-11/4/29.**G.**
Dar.30/12/29-19/2/30.**G.**
Don.6/6-17/7/31.**G.**
Don.11/7-20/8/32.**G.**
Dar.10-17/2/33.**H.**
New tyres.
Don.20/4-3/6/33.**G.**
Don.21/9-19/10/34.**G.**
Don.10/10-4/12/35.**G.**
Don.6/11-9/12/36.**G.**

Don.26/2-6/3/37.**L.**
Don.26/4-1/5/37.**L.**
Dar.5/8/37.*Weigh.*
Dar.21/10-8/11/37.**N/C.**
Don.3/1-11/2/38.**G.**
Dar.30/4-12/5/38.**N/C.**
Right Driving box hot.
Dar.27/1/39.*Weigh.*
Don.6/3-20/4/39.**G.**
Don.5/4-10/5/40.**G.**
Don.4/11/41- *Into shops for rebuilding to Class A3.*

BOILERS:
7804
7799 (ex2577) 20/6/28
7803 (ex2569) 19/2/30
7696 (ex2550) 17/7/31
7704 (exSpare) 4/12/35

TENDERS:
5292 6/12/24-2/11/36
5282 9/12/36-

SHEDS:
Heaton
Gateshead 17/6/40
Heaton 26/10/40

2559 until 28th November 1936 kept an original G.N. design railed tender and is here on an all-stations train stopping at Crow Park, between Tuxford and Newark. This typical Great Northern country station makes a very nostalgic scene, now but a memory.

2559's change of tender was interesting because it got a high-sided example which had been ordered in 1934 to run with the 2-8-2 No.2002, but which never did so, that loco getting one from the next batch built. Here at New Southgate, 2559 is on a train going to Spalding and Boston, from which it would detach at Peterborough.

4472 was the engine selected to represent the London & North Eastern Railway on their stand at the 1924 British Empire Exhibition held at Wembley, where in July that year I was duly impressed by it. Wheel rims had been polished, as had the splasher beadings and the Company's coat-of-arms adorned the cab sides. That disappeared in 1928 when corridor tender was attached, and only one further locomotive was so privileged - a mundane 4-4-0 in October 1944, so done and given green painting simply for ferrying the Southern Area's officers inspection saloon about the Area.

2744 went to Kings Cross shed and did make use of its corridor tender, although not until the 1933 season of non-stop runs. In December 1936 that tender was taken over by A4 class No.4483, and one of the coal-rail type was substituted. Then on 7th July 1937 No.2744 was transferred to Haymarket shed and from there on 10th December of that same year, came to grief at Castlecary in a blinding snowstorm, whilst on the 4 p.m. from Edinburgh to Glasgow, colliding with the rear of a Dundee to Glasgow passenger train.

2744 as received at Doncaster works on 3rd April 1938. A replacement of it was sufficiently far advanced to enter traffic on 14th April, probably carrying little, if anything, from the original construction.

This 2744 leaving Kings Cross is the replacement locomotive which was allocated to Doncaster shed, and worked mainly between there and London.

PART TWO

THE A3 CLASS

Repairs:- C/H-Casual Heavy.	C/L-Casual Light.	G-General.	H-Heavy.	H/I-Heavy Intermediate.	L-Light.	L/I-Light Intermediate.	N/C-Non-Classified.
Works:- Cow - Cowlairs. Dar - Darlington. Don - Doncaster. Gat - Gateshead. Gor - Gorton. Hay - Haymarket shed. SRX - St Rollox.

2743
FELSTEAD.

DONCASTER   1693

To traffic   22/8/28

REPAIRS:
Don.21/11/29-10/1/30.**G**
Don.25-28/2/30.**N/C.**
Don.26-31/5/30.**L.**
Don.7/5-27/6/31.**G.**
Don.27/5-14/7/32.**H.**
Don.19/5-10/7/33.**H.**
Don.1/8-1/9/34.**H.**
Don.26/8-18/10/35.**G.**
Don.29/10-13/11/35.**H.**
Don.19/10-1/12/36.**G.**
Don.30/3-3/4/37.**L.**
Don.19-20/10/37.**L.**
Don.18/1-19/2/38.**G.**
Don.4-5/3/38.**N/C.**
Don.16/3/38. *Fitted with
Stone Deuta Speed Recorder.*
Don.18/2-1/4/39.**G.**
Don.11/6-13/7/40.**G.**
Don.2/4-10/5/42.**G.**
Don.14/8-16/9/43.**G.**
Don.15-23/2/44.**N/C.**
Don.28/4-14/6/45.**G.**
Don.31/7-18/9/46.**G.**
Don.27/7-3/9/48.**G.**
Don.17/8-16/9/49.**G.**
Don.19/9-27/10/50.**G.**
Don.15-24/11/50.**N/C.**
Don.18/2-21/3/52.**G.**
Don.14/9-13/10/53.**G.**
Hay.7-16/4/54.**C/L.**
Don.15/1-18/2/55.**G.**
Don.9/8-26/9/56.**G.**
Don.12/4-21/5/58.**G.**
Don.19/8-9/10/59.**G.**
Don.28/10/59-3/3/60.**G.**
After accident.
Don.29/4-31/5/60.**C/L.**
SRx.31/1-11/2/61.**N/C.**
Don.20/9-11/10/61.**G.**

BOILERS:
8075
8253 (new) 27/6/31
8027 (ex2544) 10/7/33
8254 (ex2751) 13/11/35
8030 (ex2599) 13/7/40
9512 (new) 18/9/46
9115 (ex50) 3/9/48
27004 (new) 27/10/50
27073 (ex60070) 21/3/52
27003 (ex60086) 13/10/53
27018 (ex60048) 18/2/55
27001 (ex60078) 26/9/56
27072 (ex60077) 21/5/58
27015 (ex60082) 9/10/59

27086 (ex60112) 3/3/60
29329 (ex60071) 10/11/61

TENDERS:
5330 22/8/28-6/2/29
5255 6/2/29-7/11/57
5572 7/11/57-18/12/57
5255 18/12/57-18/11/59
5254 3/3/60-14/10/63

SHEDS:
Doncaster
Gateshead 15/3/36
Doncaster 17/7/36
Grantham 9/2/41
Kings Cross 19/5/46
Haymarket 18/2/51
Dundee 21/11/60
St Margarets 19/12/60

RENUMBERED:
No.89. 18/9/46
No.60089. 3/9/48

CONDEMNED:
14/10/63.
To Inverurie for Cut-up
2/11/63.
Completed 21/2/64.

2744
GRAND PARADE

DONCASTER   1694

To traffic   23/8/28

REPAIRS:
Don.24/9-2/10/28.**L.**
Don.11/11/29-3/1/30.**G.**
Don.24/1/30.**N/C.**
Don.21/1-14/3/31.**G.**
Don.29/1-29/3/32.**G.**
Don.23/1-8/3/33.**H.**
Don.5/3-28/4/34.**G.**
Don.9/3-10/4/35.**G.**
Don.6/3-30/4/36.**G.**
Don.2-11/12/36.**G.**
Don.14-4-8/5/37.**H.**
Don.24/8-5/10/37.**H.**
Don.2-14/4/38.**G.** *Castle-
cary smash Replacement.*
Don.4/5-17/6/39.**G.**
Don.13/8-13/9/40.**L.**
Don.17/1-22/2/41.**G.**
Don.12/12/41-10/1/42.**L.**
Don.2/10-18/11/42.**G.**
Don.20/7-1/9/44.**G.**
Don.16/10-24/11/45.**G.**
Don.23/4-24/5/47.**G.**
Don.15/1-16/2/49.**G.**
Don.25/9-1/11/50.**G.**

Don.15/4-15/5/52.**G.**
Don.30/10-14/11/52.**L.**
Don.30/3-17/4/53.**L.**
Don.18/11-18/12/53.**G.**
Don.13/4-27/5/55.**G.**
Hay.21-29/8/55.**C/L.**
Don.4/2-26/3/57.**G.**
Hay.4-11/2/58.**C/L.**
Don.16/6-8/8/58.**G.**
Don.8/7-16/9/59.**H/I.**
Don.8/3-8/5/61.**G.**
Don.19/11/62-21/1/63.**C/L.**
Don.10/7-15/8/63.**N/C.**

BOILERS:
8076
8075 (ex2743) 29/3/32
8029 (ex2580) 8/3/33
8247 (ex2595) 30/4/36
8029 (ex2544) 14/4/38
9453 (new) 1/9/44
9977 (new) 16/2/49
27006 (new) 1/11/50
27062 (ex60054) 18/12/53
27025 (ex60069) 27/5/55
27006 (ex60077) 26/3/57
27045 (ex60084) 8/8/58

TENDERS:
5331 23/8/28-29/6/29
5273 29/6/29-3/8/32
5331 3/8/32-20/1/33
5273 20/1/33-18/7/33
5331 18/7/33-2/12/36
5267 11/12/36-2/4/38.
*Engine destroyed at Castle-
cary. Replacement got tender number:-*
5263 14/4/38-15/1/49
5285 16/2/49-19/5/50
5261 19/5/50-21/7/59
5279 2/9/59-28/10/63

SHEDS:
Kings Cross
Haymarket 7/7/37
Doncaster 31/3/38
Grantham 1/7/43
New England 11/4/44
Leicester Cen 16/2/49
Grantham 16/5/49
Doncaster 2/4/50
Haymarket 2/7/50
Dundee 21/11/60
St Margarets 19/12/60
St Rollox 18/6/62
Eastfield 31/12/62
St Rollox 14/1/63

RENUMBERED:
No.90. 9/12/46
No.60090. 16/2/49

CONDEMNED:
28/10/63.
To Cowlairs for Cut-up
24/1/64.

2745
CAPTAIN CUTTLE.

DONCASTER   1695

To traffic   8/9/28

REPAIRS:
Don.10-19/10/28.**L.**
Cow.5/10-19/11/29.**G.**
Cow.11/9-11/11/30.**G.**
Cow.13/11/30.**N/C.**
Cow.24/11-23/12/30.**L.**
Cow.13-28/1/31.**L.**
Cow.16/2-3/3/31.**L.**
Cow.7-25/5/31.**L.**
Cow.16/6-2/7/31.**L.**
Cow.8-24/10/31.**L.**
Don.13/4-7/6/32.**G.**
Cow.23/8-4/10/32.**L.**
Don.16/3-9/5/33.**G.**
Don.12/10-14/11/33.**L.**
Don.25/4-26/6/34.**G.**
Don.8/3-12/4/35.**H.**
Don.13-20/8/35.**L.**
Don.8/4-30/5/36.**G.**
Cow.24/11-2/12/36.**L.**
Don.14/1-4/3/37.**H.**
Don.20/10-26/11/37.**H.**
Don.29/6-4/8/38.**G.**
Don.31/5-22/7/39.**G.**
Don.16/8-18/9/39.**L.**
Cow.22-24/5/40.**L.**
Cow.15-20/6/40.**L.**
Don.15-8-25/9/40.**G.**
Don.19/12/41-16/2/42.**G.**
Don.7/9-9/10/43.**G.**
Don.22/2-6/4/45.**G.**
Cow.23/4/46.**N/C.**
Don.26/8-11/10/46.**G.**
Don.4/2-2/4/48.**G.**
Don.14-23/4/48.**N/C.**
*Painting new colour and
inspection by C.M.E.*
Cow.6-13/12/48.**L.**
Don.31/3-14/4/49.**C/L.**
Don.27/9-3/11/49.**G.**
Don.4/4-3/5/51.**G.**
Don.3/12/52-6/1/53.**G.**
Don.18-25/9/54.**G.**
Don.29/12/55-3/2/56.**G.**
Don.15/7-23/8/57.**G.**
Don.13/6-9/7/58.**C/L.**
Don.19/1-14/3/59.**G.**
Don.8-22/5/59.**N/C.**
Don.4/8-8/10/60.**C/H.**
Don.10-13/4/61.**N/C.**

Don.4/8-11/10/61.**G.**

BOILERS:
8077
8028 (ex2544) 7/6/32
8251 (ex2749) 4/3/37
8028 (ex Spare) 22/7/39
8080 (ex2747) 6/4/45
8077 (ex2796) 2/4/48
9510 (ex2545) 3/11/49
27044 (ex60062) 3/5/51
27084 (ex60094) 6/1/53
27017 (ex60075) 25/9/54
27014 (ex60086) 3/2/56
27010 (ex60108) 23/8/57
27059 (ex60070) 11/10/61

TENDERS:
5332 8/9/28-30/6/30
5480 30/6/30-12/10/64

SHEDS:
Doncaster
Haymarket 24/10/28
Carlisle 26/10/28
Gateshead 30/5/48
Heaton 13/6/48
Gateshead 6/7/58
Darlington 7/6/59
Gateshead 6/12/59
Darlington 17/12/61
Gateshead 24/6/62
Heaton 9/9/62
Gateshead 16/6/63

RENUMBERED:
No.91. 10/10/46
No.60091. 2/4/48

CONDEMNED:
12/10/64.
Sold for scrap to A. Draper,
Hull 12/64.

2746
FAIRWAY.

DONCASTER   1700

To traffic   26/10/28

REPAIRS:
Don.10/2-27/3/30.**G.**
Don.4/3-18/4/31.**G.**
Don.3/6-16/7/32.**G.**
Don.9/2-13/4/33.**H.**
Don.9/2-31/3/34.**G.**
Don.14/2-21/3/35.**G.**
Don.8-13/7/35.**L.**
Don.24/10-12/11/35.**L.**
Don.28/1-28/3/36.**G.**
Don.20-22/4/36.**L.**
Don.28/4-10/5/36.**L.**
Don.11/3-24/4/37.**G.**
Don.25/10-24/11/37.**L.**
Don.22/4-2/6/38.**G.**
Don.20/6-12/8/39.**G.**
Don.18/11-28/12/40.**G.**
Don.25/4-9/7/42.**G.**
Don.11/8-23/9/44.**G.**
Don.27/2-30/3/46.**G.**
Don.8/5-14/6/47.**G.**

Don.1/3-13/4/49.**G.**
Don.17/10-17/11/50.**G.**
Don.28/11-1/12/50.**N/C.**
Don.16/7-19/8/52.**G.**
Don.27/10-3/12/53.**G.**
Don.10/2-17/3/55.**G.**
Don.2/5-11/7/56.**G.**
Don.12-21/11/56.**N/C.**
Don.11/12/57-10/1/58.**G.**
Don.11-19/6/58.**N/C.**
Don.7-27/2/59.**C/L.**
Don.1/10-13/11/59.**G.**
Don.17/2-11/3/61.**C/L.**
Don.3-12/4/61.**C/L.**
Don.18/9-25/10/61.**G.**
Don.2-8/11/61.**N/C.**

BOILERS:
8078
8030 (ex2573) 16/7/32
8720 (new) 21/3/35
8083 (ex Spare) 12/8/39
9485 (new) 30/3/46
27011 (new) 17/11/50
27042 (ex60073) 3/12/53
27003 (ex60089) 17/3/55
27084 (ex60050) 10/1/58
27079 (ex60040) 13/11/59
29272 (ex60050) 25/10/61

TENDERS:
5265 26/10/28-30/6/29
5326 30/6/29-11/3/37
5642 24/4/37-25/10/37
5574 24/11/37-12/10/64

SHEDS:
Kings Cross
Gateshead 10/11/36
Kings Cross 15/12/36
Gateshead 14/1/37
Heaton 28/3/43
Holbeck 8/5/60
Ardsley 11/6/61
Gateshead 16/6/63

RENUMBERED:
No.92. 27/10/46
No.60092. 13/4/49

CONDEMNED:
12/10/64.
Sold for scrap to A. Draper,
Hull 12/64

2747
CORONACH

Doncaster   1703

To traffic 24/11/28

REPAIRS:
Don.26/6-18/7/29.**H.**
Don.5/6-26/7/30.**G.**
Don.14/9-17/10/31.**G.**
Don.8/12/32-6/2/33.**G.**
Don.12-22/5/33.**G.**
Don.18/1-10/3/34.**H.**
Don.13/3-20/4/35.**G.**
Don.14/5-26/6/36.**G.**
Don.9-13/11/36.**L.**

Don.31/8-9/10/37.**G.**
Don.4-14/4/38.**L.**
Don.8/12/38-23/1/39.**G.**
Don.19/3-4/5/40.**G.**
Don.16/7-30/8/41.**G.**
Don.15/1-28/2/42.**G.**
Don.10/3-28/4/44.**G.**
Don.7/1-6/2/46.**G.**
Don.7/7-8/8/47.**G.**
Don.3-9/10/47.**L.**
Don.1-19/11/48.**L.**
Don.20/1-3/2/49.**L.**
Don.31/8-14/10/49.**G.**
Don.9-21/6/50.**L.**
Don.15/1-16/2/51.**G.**
Don.7/4-7/5/52.**G.**
Don.8-22/12/52.**L.**
Don.7/1-11/2/54.**G.**
Don.20/4-2/5/55.**C/L.**
Don.11/8-23/9/55.**G.**
Don.2/4-17/5/57.**G.**
Don.8/11-19/12/58.**G.**
Don.25/10-2/12/60.**G.**
Don.4/12/61-6/1/62.**C/L**

BOILERS:
8079
8082 (ex2751) 17/10/31
8075 (ex2744) 22/5/33
8080 (ex2580) 26/6/36
9448 (new) 28/4/44
9511 (ex36) 14/10/49. *9511
re-numbered 27031 16/2/51*
27004 (ex60089) 7/5/52
27026 (ex60099) 11/2/54
27031 (ex60062) 23/9/55
27074 (ex60061) 19/12/58
29322 (ex60066) 2/12/60

TENDERS:
5226 24/11/28-10/9/31
5272 10/9/31-13/3/35
5280 20/4/35-4/4/38
5223 14/4/38-3/5/38
5280 15/6/38-8/12/38
5286 23/1/39-15/1/42
5275 28/2/42-7/4/52
5287 7/5/52-24/4/62

SHEDS:
Doncaster
Kings Cross 17/3/30
Doncaster 31/5/30
Haymarket 16/3/39
Carlisle 23/1/41

RENUMBERED:
No.93. 7/7/46
No.60093. 19/9/48

CONDEMNED:
24/4/62.
Cut-up Doncaster Works.

2748
COLORADO

Doncaster   1705

To traffic 20/12/28

REPAIRS:*
Don.4/4-23/5/31.**G.**
Don.11/1-10/3/32.**H.**
Don.11-13/5/32.**L.**
Don.20/3-13/5/33.**G.**
Don.22-26/6/33.**N/C.**
Don.23/3-4/5/34.**N/C.**
Don.1/8-1/9/34.**G.**
Don.14/11-20/12/34.**H.**
Don.29/6-13/7/35.**H.**
Don.7-26/11/35.**G.**
Don.14/5-26/6/36.**G.**
Don.12/4-24/5/37.**G.**
Don.22/10-3/12/37.**H.**
Don.20/7-24/8/38.**G.**
Don.24/6-12/8/39.**G.**
Cow.29/5/40.**L.**
Don.18/7-29/8/40.**G.**
Don.16/5-18/6/41.**G.**
Don.18/8-16/10/41.**H.**
Cow.10-18/8/42.**L.**
Don.13/4-28/5/43.**G.**
Cow.2-5/8/44.**L.**
Don.18/6-2/8/45.**G.**
Don.25/7-26/9/47.**G.**
Don.6/11-20/12/48.**G.**
Don.28/3-10/5/50.**G.**
Don.15-18/5/50.**N/C.**
Don.25/3-29/4/52.**G.**
Don.14/10-20/11/53.**G.**
Don.15/3-21/4/55.**G.**
Don.22/2-7/4/56.**H/I.**
Hay.6-16/10/56.**C/L.**
Hay.18-22/3/57.**C/L.**
Don.2/10-22/11/57.**G.**
Hay.5-14/3/58.**C/L.**
Don.9/12/58-1/1/59.**N/C.**
Don.22/7-26/8/59.**G.**
Don.5/7-16/8/61.**G.**
Don.11/12/62-28/1/63.**C/L.**
Don.31/1-19/2/63.**N/C.**
Don.4/7-4/9/63.**C/H.**

BOILERS:
8080
8077 (ex2745) 10/3/32
8225 (ex2597) 1/9/34
8078 (ex2796) 3/12/37
8225 (exSpare) 12/8/39
9118 (ex2597) 26/9/47
9568 (ex67) 10/5/50
27076 (ex60052) 29/4/52
27013 (ex60067) 21/4/55
27034 (ex60076) 22/11/57
27014 (ex60039) 26/8/59
27962 (ex60030) 16/8/61

TENDERS:
5271 20/12/28-18/8/41
5279 16/10/41-25/7/59
5261 26/8/59-10/12/62
5567 10/12/62-24/2/64

SHEDS:
Doncaster
Kings Cross 13/2/29
Carlisle 5/4/29
Haymarket 29/12/47
St Margarets 13/12/61
St Rollox 18/6/62
Eastfield 31/12/62
St Rollox 14/1/63

Repairs:- **C/H**-Casual Heavy. **C/L**-Casual Light. **G**-General. **H**-Heavy. **H/I**-Heavy Intermediate. **L**-Light. **L/I**-Light Intermediate. **N/C**-Non-Classified.
Works:- Cow - Cowlairs. Dar - Darlington. Don - Doncaster. Gat - Gateshead. Gor - Gorton. Hay - Haymarket shed. SRX - St Rollox.

34

RENUMBERED:
No.94. 1/12/46
No.60094. 20/12/48

CONDEMNED:
24/2/64
Sold for scrap 6/64 to
Henderson's of Airdrie.

The first Engine History Cards of both 2748 and 2749 were, like A1 2567, lost during re-organisation in the early BR period.

2749
FLAMINGO

Doncaster   1707

To traffic   26/1/29

REPAIRS:*
Don.26/5-26/6/31.**H.**
Don.25/2-23/4/32.**G.**
Don.6-25/6/32.**H.**
Don.31/10-14/11/32.**L.**
Don.11/5-28/6/33.**G.**
Don.8/6-5/7/34.**G.**
Don.23/5-29/6/35.**G.**
Don.7-28/3/36.**G.**
Don.4/6-16/7/36.**H.**
Don.14/4-22/5/37.**G.**
Don.9/6-8/7/38.**G.**
Don.22/4-3/6/39.**G.**
Cow.16-18/5/40.**L.**
Don.7/12/40-25/1/41.**G.**
Don.27/10-23/11/41.**L.**
Don.12/10-9/12/42.**G.**
Cow.27/1-2/2/43.**L.**
Don.13-27/2/43.**L.**
Don.4/5-10/6/44.**G.**
Don.6-22/12/44.**L.**
Don.9/2-16/3/46.**G.**
Don.13-27/4/46.**L.**
Don.21/7-29/8/47.**G.**
Don.7/1-11/2/49.**G.**
Don.10/11-15/12/50.**G.**
Don.28/4-28/5/52.**G.**
Don.18/1-19/2/54.**G.**
Don.28/7-2/9/55.**G.**
Don.25/5-13/7/57.**G.**
Don.23/12/58-6/2/59.**G.**
Don.1/4/61- *Not repaired.*

BOILERS:
8081
8251 (ex4480) 28/6/33
8031 (exSpare) 16/7/36
8247 (ex2744) 8/7/38
9450 (New) 10/6/44
8781 (ex2560) 11/2/49
27017 (ex60108) 15/12/50
27023 (ex60096) 28/5/52
29307 (exSpare) 19/2/54
29283 (ex60013) 13/7/57
29299 (ex60085) 6/2/59

TENDERS:
5255 26/1/29-6/2/29
5330 6/2/29-20/3/29
5275 20/3/29-9/6/38
5224 8/7/38-18/1/54
5637 19/2/54-10/4/61

SHEDS:
Doncaster
Carlisle 6/2/29

RENUMBERED:
No.558. 13/3/46
No.95. 5/5/46
No.60095. 19/9/48

CONDEMNED:
10/4/61.
Cut-up Doncaster.

2750
PAPYRUS

Doncaster   1708

To traffic   23/2/29

REPAIRS:
Don.23/9-24/10/29.**N/C.**
Don.11/4-30/5/30.**G.**
Don.21-23/10/30.**N/C.**
Don.29/4-13/6/31.**G.**
Don.24/6-10/8/32.**G.**
Don.6/10-18/11/33.**G.**
Don.29/11/34-19/1/35.**G.**
Don.22-27/2/35.**L.**
Don.10-18/4/35.**L.**
Don.18-24/6/35.**L.**
Don.8/1-26/2/36.**G.**
Don.14/5-2/6/36.**H.**
Don.28/9-7/10/36.**L.**
Don.13-27/11/36.**H.**
Don.19/4-4/6/37.**G.**
Don.6-7/9/37.**N/C.**
Tender change only.
Don.21-22/10/37.**L.**
Alteration to Blow-down.
Don.18/5-18/6/38.**G.**
Don.12-15/12/38.**L.**
Don.3/10-18/11/39.**G.**
Don.26/7-2/8/40.**L.**
Don.24/6-2/8/41.**G.**
Don.6/4-8/5/43.**G.**
Don.17-20/5/43.**N/C.**
Don.21/10-29/11/44.**G.**
Don.28/3-16/5/46.**G.**
Don.7/11-15/12/47.**G.**
Don.12-27/10/48.**H/I.**
Don.18/7-25/8/49.**G.**
Don.1-12/12/49.**L.**
Don.5/12/50-11/1/51.**G.**
Don.3/3-3/4/52.**G.**
Don.8/10-12/11/53.**G.**
Hay.3-24/5/54.**C/L.**
Don.18/3-22/4/55.**G.**
Don.21/10-21/11/55.**C/L.**
Don.17/8-11/10/56.**G.**
Don.22/5-23/7/58.**G.**
Don.8-18/4/59.**C/L.**
Don.10/12/59-23/1/60.**G.**
Don.29/7-15/9/61.**G.**

BOILERS:
8083
8253 (ex2743) 18/11/33
8075 (exSpare) 18/6/38
9216 (New) 8/5/43
8784 (ex2554) 15/12/47
9985 (New) 25/8/49
27023 (ex60047) 11/1/51
27075 (ex60103) 3/4/52

27072 (ex60037) 12/11/53
27065 (ex60053) 22/4/55
27076 (ex60042) 11/10/56
27009 (ex60072) 23/7/58
27069 (ex60046) 23/1/60
27014 (ex60094) 15/9/61

TENDERS:
5273 23/2/29-29/6/29
5331 29/6/29-24/6/32
5273 10/8/32-20/1/33
5331 20/1/33-18/7/33
5225 18/7/33-24/8/34
5327 24/8/34-13/11/36
5292 27/11/36-30/6/37
5329 30/6/37-6/9/37
5581 7/9/37-8/10/53
5270 12/11/53-9/9/63

SHEDS:
Kings Cross
Haymarket 14/8/37
Kings Cross 8/9/37
Doncaster 12/10/37
Grantham 11/3/39
Kings Cross 27/10/46
Haymarket 2/7/50
St Margarets 13/12/61

RENUMBERED:
No.96. 11/11/46
No.60096. 27/10/48

CONDEMNED:
9/9/63.
Sold to Arnott Young,
Carmyle 6/64 for scrap.

2751
HUMORIST

Doncaster   1709

To traffic   7/3/29

REPAIRS:
Don.8/1-22/2/30.**H.**
Don.24/3-14/5/31.**G.**
Don.29/2-22/4/32.**H.**
Don.1-5/11/32.**L.**
Don.8/2-30/3/33.**G.**
Don.7-8/4/33.**N/C.**
Don.25/5/33.**N/C.**
Don.8/11/33-8/1/34.**H.**
Don.26/2-10/4/35.**G.**
Don.13-16/4/35.**N/C.**
Don.25/5-4/7/36.**G.**
Don.20/7/36.**L.**
Don.26/6-30/7/37.**G.**
Don.1-3/11/37.**L.**
Don.3-11/2/38.**L.**
Don.13/5/38.**L.**
Don.30/9-29/10/38.**G.**
Don.30/9-23/11/39.**G.**
Don.26/2-29/3/41.**G.**
Don.8/7-7/8/42.**G.**
Don.8/2-20/3/43.**L.**
Don.26/4-27/5/44.**G.**
Don.1-8/7/44.**L.**
Don.14/5-8/6/45.**G.**
Don.8/8-26/9/46.**G.**
Don.21-25/4/47.**L.**
Don.12/5-24/6/48.**G.**
Don.24/10-30/11/49.**G.**
Don.20/3-19/4/51.**G.**

Don.14/10-20/11/52.**H/I.**
Hay.16/2-10/3/54.**C/L.**
Don.5/5-10/6/54.**G.**
Don.12/12/55-31/1/56.**G.**
Don.29/7-19/9/57.**G.**
Don.18/11-23/12/58.**G.**
Don.13/7-2/9/60.**G.**
Don.29/12/61-9/2/62.**G.**
Don.16/10-29/11/62.**C/L.**

BOILERS:
8082
8254 (New) 14/5/31
8077 (ex Static boiler at
Plant steam shed) 10/4/35
8252 (ex2596) 29/3/41
9516 (New) 26/9/46
27041 (ex60087) 19/4/51
27020 (ex60069) 10/6/54
27079 (ex60075) 31/1/56
27044 (ex60066) 19/9/57
27067 (ex60053) 23/12/58
27044 (ex60103) 2/9/60
29339 (ex60043) 9/2/62

TENDERS:
5274 7/3/29-10/8/29
5265 10/8/29-24/8/63

SHEDS:
Doncaster
Grantham 7/8/42
Kings Cross 27/10/46
Haymarket 2/7/50
Carlisle Canal 6/1/54
Haymarket 21/2/54
St Margarets 13/12/61

RENUMBERED:
No.97. 27/5/46
No.60097. 24/6/48

CONDEMNED:
24/8/63, after entering
Doncaster Works for repair
23/7/63. Cut-up Doncaster.

2752
SPION KOP

Doncaster   1710

To traffic   20/4/29

REPAIRS:
Don.4/3-12/4/30.**H.**
Don.26/5-15/7/31.**G.**
Don.7/7-18/8/32.**G.**
Don.29/12/33-17/2/34.**G.**
Don.12/4-23/5/35.**G.**
Don.2-31/12/35.**H.**
After Collision.
Don.7/12/36-23/1/37.**G.**
Don.22/2-3/3/37.**H.**
Don.27/9-28/10/37.**G.**
Don.26/7-3/9/38.**G.**
Don.28/10-2/12/39.**G.**
Don.17/5-8/6/40.**L.**
Don.6/6-18/7/41.**G.**
Don.23/12/42-24/2/43.**G.**
Don.2-19/7/44.**G.**
Don.20/9-3/10/44.**L.**
Don.22/11/45-4/1/46.**G.**
Don.16/1-1/3/47.**G.**

Don.17/9-3/11/48.**G.**
Don.19/6-28/7/50.**G.**
Don.22/10-24/11/52.**G.**
Cow.11-23/1/54.**N/C.**
Hay.3-10/8/54.**C/L.**
Don.16/12/54-28/1/55.**G.**
Hay.25-28/7/55.**C/L.**
Don.26/9-1/11/55.**C/L.**
Don.15/8-18/10/56.**G.**
Don.28/2-1/4/58.**G.**
Don.10-19/12/58.**N/C.**
Don.1/6-17/7/59.**G.**
Don.15/4-25/5/61.**G.**

BOILERS:
8084
8076 (ex2744) 18/8/32
8081 (ex2597) 23/5/35
8031 (ex2749) 3/9/38
8254 (ex2743) 18/7/41
9210 (ex2558) 3/11/48
9445 (ex40) 28/7/50. *9445 renumbered 27082 24/11/52.*
27018 (ex60089) 18/10/56
27049 (ex60069) 1/4/58
27023 (ex60111) 17/7/59
29304 (ex60027) 25/5/61

TENDERS:
5326 20/4/29-30/6/29
5272 30/6/29-10/9/31
5226 10/9/31-7/12/36
5638 23/1/37-27/9/37
5580 28/10/37-26/7/38
5267 3/9/38-23/12/42
5481 24/2/43-28/10/63

SHEDS:
Doncaster
Haymarket 29/1/38
St Margarets 8/2/38
Doncaster 2/3/38
Grantham 1/7/43
New England 2/4/44
Grantham 16/4/44
New England 29/5/44
Kings Cross 18/8/46
Doncaster 4/6/50
Haymarket 6/8/50
St Margarets 6/1/63

RENUMBERED:
No.561. 18/3/46
No.98. 2/6/46
No.60098. 3/11/48

CONDEMNED:
28/10/63.
Into Inverurie Works for
cut-up 7/2/64.

2595
TRIGO

Doncaster   1731

To traffic   22/2/30

REPAIRS:
Don.10/4-28/5/31.**G.**
Don.18/5-5/7/32.**G.**
Don.19/5-26/6/33.**G.**

Don.12-20/12/33.**L.**
Don.17/11/34-2/1/35.**G.**
Don.19-26/1/35.**N/C.**
Don.30/10-13/12/35.**G.**
Don.12/11-19/12/36.**G.**
Don.16/9-22/10/37.**G.**
Don.14/10-25/11/38.**G.**
Don.18/10-19/11/39.**G.**
Don.14/10-28/11/40.**G.**
Don.2-22/3/42.**L.**
Don.20/8-3/10/42.**G.**
Don.23/11-31/12/43.**G.**
Don.11-26/5/44.**L.**
Don.21/2-15/3/45.**L.**
Don.4/8-6/10/45.**G.**
Don.31/12/46-1/2/47.**G.**
Don.26-27/2/47.**N/C.**
Don.10/11-18/12/47.**G.**
Don.3-14/1/48.**L.**
Don.19-31/5/48.**L.**
Don.20/4-1/6/49.**G.**
Don.21/2-29/3/51.**G.**
Don.5-22/6/51.**L.**
Don.8/7-8/8/52.**G.**
Don.11-17/11/52.**N/C.**
Don.8-27/1/53.**L.**
Don.29/12/53-28/1/54.**G.**
Don.12/4-27/5/55.**G.**
Don.30/8-27/10/56.**G.**
Don.14-28/5/57.**C/L.**
Don.21/5-10/7/58.**G.**
Don.6/11-9/12/59.**G.**
Don.20-22/9/60.**N/C.**
Don.8/12/61-18/1/62.**G.**

BOILERS:
8223
8247 (ex2796) 26/6/33
8084 (ex2596) 13/12/35
8720 (exSpare) 28/11/40
9567 (New) 1/2/47
27036 (ex60045) 29/3/51
27016 (ex60075) 8/8/52
27073 (ex60089) 28/1/54
27072 (ex60096) 27/5/55
27045 (ex60112) 27/10/56
27026 (ex60112) 10/7/58
27076 (ex60053) 9/12/59
27001 (ex60035) 18/1/62

TENDERS:
5476 22/2/30-14/10/40
5645 28/11/40-23/11/64

SHEDS:
Gateshead
Heaton 28/3/43
Gateshead 3/11/45
Neville Hill 4/9/49
Gateshead 8/12/63

RENUMBERED:
No.84. 27/10/46
No.60084. 31/5/48

CONDEMNED:
23/11/64.
Sold for scrap to Hughes
Bolckow, North Blyth 1/65.

2596
MANNA

Doncaster   1733

To traffic   22/2/30

REPAIRS:
Don.30/11/31-18/1/32.**G.**
Don.17/1-3/3/33.**G.**
Don.27/12/33-15/2/34.**G.**
Don.14/8-22/9/34.**H.**
Don.23/5-29/6/35.**G.**
Don.20/5-8/7/36.**G.**
Don.5/2-19/3/37.**G.**
Don.10/12/37-14/1/38.**G.**
Don.16/2-8/3/38.**L.**
After collision.
Don.18/1-18/2/39.**G.**
Don.6/2-26/3/40.**G.**
Don.6/8-14/9/41.**G.**
Don.2/3-2/4/43.**G.**
Don.5-21/1/44.**L.**
Don.21/10-18/11/44.**G.**
Don.24/1-23/2/46.**G.**
Don.18/11-24/12/47.**G.**
Don.3/10-11/11/49.**G.**
Don.21-24/11/49.**N/C.**
Don.29/11-1/12/49.**N/C.**
Don.15/5-14/6/51.**G.**
Don.24/11-23/12/52.**G.**
Don.24/3-29/4/54.**G.**
Don.28/9-11/11/55.**G.**
Don.10/5-20/6/57.**G.**
Don.26/9-5/11/58.**G.**
Don.21/10-11/11/59.**C/L.**
Don.25/4-8/6/60.**G.**
Don.12/3-27/4/62.**G.**

BOILERS:
8224
8084 (ex2752) 3/3/33
8252 (ex2573) 29/6/35
8253 (ex Static boiler at
Plant steam shed) 26/3/40
9215 (New) 2/4/43
8249 (ex59) 11/11/49
27048 (ex60042) 14/6/51
27015 (ex60103) 29/4/54
29299 (ex60021) 11/11/55
29279 (ex60066) 5/11/58
29318 (ex60006) 8/6/60
27039 (ex60107) 27/4/62

TENDERS:
5477 22/2/30-5/2/37
5483 19/3/37-24/1/46
5643 23/2/46-15/3/46
5483 15/3/46-12/3/62
5283 27/4/62-12/10/64

SHEDS:
Gateshead
Heaton 28/3/43
Gateshead 14/2/44
Heaton 31/8/44
Gateshead 16/6/63

RENUMBERED:
No.85. 27/10/46
No.60085. 3/7/48

CONDEMNED:
12/10/64.
Sold for scrap to A. Draper,
Hull 12/64.

2597
GAINSBOROUGH

Doncaster   1736

To traffic   7/4/30

REPAIRS:
Don.13/5-2/7/31.**G.**
Don.9/6-21/7/32.**G.**
Don.31/10-16/12/33.**G.**
Don.10/1-14/2/35.**G.**
Dar.25/10-7/11/35.**L.**
Don.6/1-20/2/36.**G.**
Don.14-16/6/36.**N/C.**
For trials.
Don.26/2-17/4/37.**G.**
Don.28/1-5/3/38.**G.**
Don.2-8/8/38.**L.**
Don.21/3-6/5/39.**G.**
Don.12/10-6/11/39.**L.**
Don.12/7-17/8/40.**G.**
Don.8/5-13/6/42.**G.**
Don.18/2-18/3/44.**G.**
Don.8-24/6/44.**L.**
Don.20/7-15/9/45.**G.**
Don.23/4-23/5/47.**G.**
Don.7-11/11/47.**L.**
Don.30/3-13/5/49.**G.**
Don.1-26/1/51.**G.**
Don.20/2-2/3/51.**N/C.**
Don.6/5-18/6/52.**G.**
Don.12/8-24/9/53.**G.**
Don.16-25/3/54.**N/C.**
Don.11/10-8/11/54.**C/H.**
Don.22/12/54-29/1/55.**C/L.**
Don.29/8-12/10/55.**G.**
Don.4-22/12/56.**C/L.**
Don.11/11-19/12/57.**G.**
Don.7-17/10/58.**C/L.**
Don.30/4-12/6/59.**G.**
Don.25/11/60-6/1/61.**G.**
Don.17-20/1/61.**N/C.**

BOILERS:
8225
8081 (ex2749) 16/12/33
8721 (New) 14/2/35
9118 (New) 17/8/40
8776 (ex2797) 23/5/47
9213 (ex100) 13/5/49
27027 (ex60064) 26/1/51
27003 (ex60080) 18/6/52
27014 (ex60078) 24/9/53
27074 (ex60103) 12/10/55
27046 (ex60075) 19/12/57
27052 (ex60109) 12/6/59
29317 (ex60054) 6/1/61

TENDERS:
5478 5/4/30-18/11/63

SHEDS:
Gateshead
Doncaster 15/3/36
Gateshead 17/7/36

| Repairs:- | C/H-Casual Heavy. | C/L-Casual Light. | G-General. | H-Heavy. | H/I-Heavy Intermediate. | L-Light. | L/I-Light Intermediate. | N/C-Non-Classified. |

Works:- Cow - Cowlairs. Dar - Darlington. Don - Doncaster. Gat - Gateshead. Gor - Gorton. Hay - Haymarket shed. SRX - St Rollox.

2748 worked its first three months between Doncaster and London, but on 5th April 1929 was transferred to Carlisle and for the next eighteen years, simply shuttled to and from Edinburgh. Having completed yet another of those trips, it has detached, and is closely following its empty train north out of Carlisle (Citadel) station.

2749 made up the trio of A3s sent when almost new to Carlisle to relieve the hard-pressed N.B. Atlantics from the heavier trains on the punishing pair of Waverley Route summits to be surmounted in both directions. When 2749 went to the Scottish Area on 6th February 1929 the opportunity was taken to transfer the corridor tender not required by 2743, and on 20th March Haymarket shed exchanged it with that on 2565. Here at Portobello, 2749 is getting into its stride on the up 'Thames-Forth' express bound for Carlisle and London (St Pancras). 2749 remained a Carlisle engine through to its withdrawal 32 years later.

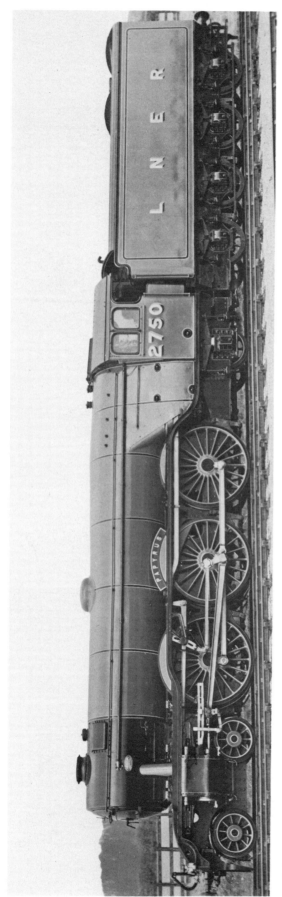

Indisputably 2750 was the first British locomotive to run at more than 100 miles per hour. It also provided the basic design for following locomotives which attained that speed reliably and regularly, and made possible a four-hour service on the 268 miles between London and Newcastle. This 18th April 1935 photograph shows it as prepared for the test run on which 108 m.p.h. was achieved

Eight more A3s were built in 1930 numbered 2595-2599 and 2795-2797 and all initially had high-sided but non-corridor type tender. 2596 also took over the name discarded when A1 class 2553 changed to *PRINCE OF WALES*.

2796 - along with 2795/7 went to Haymarket shed and did all their work from Scottish sheds. From June 1930, Nos.2795 *CALL BOY* and 2796 *SPEARMINT* were coupled with corridor tender and were regularly seen each summer in London until 1936, when these tenders went to A4s.

2797 *CICERO* at Dalmeny bringing empty stock south. It retained a high-sided non-corridor tender throughout, so apart from Doncaster works visits was rarely seen south of Newcastle and much of its work was done north and west of Edinburgh.

Heaton 30/9/39
Neville Hill 2/12/39
York 29/2/40
Heaton 28/3/43
Gateshead 30/11/44
Neville Hill 6/2/49

RENUMBERED:
No.86. 27/10/46
No.60086. 16/9/48

CONDEMNED:
18/11/63.
Into Darlington Works for
cut-up 31/12/63.

2598
BLENHEIM

Doncaster   1743

To traffic   14/6/30

REPAIRS:
Don.8/10-13/11/31.**G.**
Don.3/10-18/11/32.**G.**
Don.12/10-24/11/33.**G.**
Don.22/11/34-7/1/35.**G.**
Don.28/11/35-24/1/36.**G.**
Don.1/9-21/10/36.**G.**
Don.31/5-10/7/37.**G.**
Don.17/11-15/12/37.**H.**
Don.26-27/4/38.**L.**
Don.29/11/38-17/1/39.**G.**
Don.8/3-3/5/40.**G.**
Don.21/8-5/10/41.**G.**
Cow.12-29/5/42.**H/I.**
Don.23/9-21/10/42.**G.**
Don.9/5-10/6/44.**G.**
Don.20/8-4/10/45.**G.**
Don.28/2-21/3/46.**H.**
Don.23/12/46-17/1/47.**G.**
Don.16/5-26/6/47.**H.**
Don.30/8-20/10/48.**G.**
Don.11/7-17/8/50.**G.**
Don.28/5-4/7/52.**G.**
Don.25/11/53-4/1/54.**G.**
Don.14/12/54-11/1/55.**C/L.**
Don.28/7-2/9/55.**G.**
Don.9/10-16/11/56.**G.**
Don.15/11-4/12/57.**C/L.**
Don.1/7-12/8/58.**G.**
Don.21/12/59-3/2/60.**G.**
Don.31/5-19/7/60.**C/L.**
Don.14/12/61-2/2/62.**G.**

BOILERS:
8249
8078 (ex2746) 18/11/32
8079 (ex2580) 7/1/35
8250 (ex2599) 21/10/36
9449 (new) 10/6/44
9121 (ex53) 17/8/50
27027 (ex60086) 4/7/52
27050 (ex60079) 16/11/56
27006 (ex60090) 12/8/58
29309 (exSB960)* 3/2/60
29306 (ex60046) 2/2/62
*Boiler 9019 was used on A4
4495 from 9/43 to 6/48, was
Spare until 3/49 when it
became Static Boiler No.960

and from 12/51 worked at
Plant steam shed. In 9/59 it
was transferred back to Loco
stock and in 1/60 was renumbered 29309.

TENDERS:
5482 14/6/30-1/9/36
5572 21/10/36-7/11/57
5255 7/11/57-18/12/57
5572 18/12/57-28/10/63

SHEDS:
Gateshead
Doncaster 29/7/37
Gateshead 13/10/37
Haymarket 16/10/37
Gateshead 8/2/38
Haymarket 9/3/39
Aberdeen 20/7/40
Haymarket 18/10/41
St Margarets 13/7/60
Haymarket 28/11/60
St Margarets 13/12/61

RENUMBERED:
No.565. 21/3/46
No.87. 27/10/46
No.60087. 20/10/48

CONDEMNED:
28/10/63.
Sold for scrap to Arnott
Young, Carmyle 6/64.

2599
BOOK LAW

Doncaster   1744

To traffic   12/7/30

REPAIRS:
Don.4/9-17/10/31.**G.**
Don.4/10-25/11/32.**G.**
Don.14-16/12/32.**N/C.**
Don.17/10-6/12/33.**G.**
Don.28/12/34-1/2/35.**G.**
Don.21/11/35-4/1/36.**G.**
Don.1/10-7/11/36.**G.**
Don.16/8-18/9/37.**G.**
Don.28/4/38.**L.**
Don.7/10-12/11/38.**G.**
Don.8/6-11/7/39.**L.**
Don.11/12/39-27/1/40.**G.**
Don.13/5-27/6/41.**G.**
Don.8/2-11/3/43.**G.**
Don.9/10-10/11/44.**G.**
Don.28/11/45-10/1/46.**G.**
Don.22/7-2/8/46.**L.**
Don.8/5-12/6/47.**G.**
Don.19/1-25/2/49.**G.**
Don.19/1-10/2/50.**C/L.**
Don.9/2-14/3/51.**H/I.**
Don.19/3-10/4/52.**C/L.**
Don.7-11/2/53.**G.**
Ghd.1-3/3/54.**C/L.**
Don.30/8-14/10/54.**G.**
Don.10/10-4/11/55.**C/L.**
Don.17/1-2/3/56.**G.**
Don.17/8-27/9/57.**G.**
Don.28/7-21/8/58.**G.**

Don.14/4-1/7/59.**G.**
Don.22/4-9/6/61.**G.**

BOILERS:
8250
8223 (ex2595) 6/12/33
8250 (exSpare) 1/2/35
8030 (ex2746) 4/1/36
8081 (exSpare) 27/1/40
8250 (ex2598) 10/11/44
9209 (ex2568) 15/7/48. *9209
renumbered 27035 14/3/51.*
27058 (ex60038) 11/2/53
27084 (ex60091) 14/10/54
27004 (ex60056) 2/3/56
27075 (ex60043) 27/9/57
27064 (ex60108) 1/7/59
27016 (ex60067) 9/6/61

TENDERS:
5483 12/7/30-1/10/36
5569 7/11/36-8/2/43
5285 11/3/43-19/1/49
5263 25/2/49-15/5/63
5291 15/5/63-14/10/63

SHEDS:
Gateshead
Haymarket 8/10/37
Gateshead 23/1/38
Heaton 28/3/43
Gateshead 3/5/43
Heaton 3/11/45
Holbeck 8/5/60
Heaton 16/7/61
Gateshead 16/6/63

RENUMBERED:
No.88. 2/8/46
No.60088. 15/7/48

CONDEMNED:
14/10/63.
Into Darlington Works for
cut-up 15/11/63.

2795
CALL BOY

Doncaster   1738

To traffic   19/4/30

REPAIRS:
Don.12/2-4/3/31.**L.**
Don.26/5-2/7/31.**G.**
Dar.7-19/11/31.**L.**
Don.22/4-9/6/32.**G.**
Don.28/3-24/5/33.**H.**
Don.26/4-16/6/34.**G.**
Don.26/2-27/4/35.**H.**
Don.7/4-29/5/36.**H.**
Don.15/4-31/5/37.**G.**
Don.25/4-4/6/38.**G.**
Don.4/9-20/10/39.**G.**
Hudd ATC fitted.
Don.3/10-8/11/40.**G.**
Don.6/11-20/12/41.**G.**
Don.13/4-14/5/43.**G.**
Don.16-24/2/44.**N/C.**
Don.7/9-14/10/44.**G.**
Don.21/11-22/12/45.**G.**

Don.24/7-16/8/46.**L/I.**
Don.6/1-15/2/47.**G.**
Don.28/1-5/3/48.**G.**
Don.8/6-21/7/49.**G.**
Don.18/12/50-23/1/51.**G.**
Don.21/5-1/7/52.**G.**
Don.10/12/53-20/1/54.**G.**
Don.27/5-14/7/55.**G.**
Don.11/12/56-25/1/57.**G.**
Don.9/6-29/7/58.**G.**
Don.28/10-5/12/59.**G.**
Don.30-31/12/60.**N/C.**
Don.31/12/60-3/1/61.**N/C.**
Don.19/4-1/7/61.**G.**

BOILERS:
8226
8083 (ex2750) 16/6/34
8079 (ex2598) 31/5/37
8223 (ex2797) 14/5/43
9982 (New) 21/7/49
27025 (ex60059) 23/1/51
27026 (ex60040) 1/7/52
29317 (ex60019) 20/1/54
29306 (ex60021) 29/7/58
29281 (ex60055) 5/12/59
27064 (ex60088) 1/7/61

TENDERS:
5479 19/4/30-17/6/30
5328 17/6/30-15/4/37
5232 31/5/37-16/2/44
5568 24/2/44-28/10/63

SHEDS:
Haymarket
St Margarets 12/1/40
Haymarket 19/10/40
St Margarets 6/1/63

RENUMBERED:
No.99. 21/7/46
No.E99. 5/3/48
No.60099. 21/7/49

CONDEMNED:
28/10/63.
Sold for scrap to Arnott
Young, Carmyle 6/64.

2796
SPEARMINT

Doncaster   1741

To traffic   17/5/30

REPAIRS:
Don.1/4-16/5/31.**G.**
Don.10/5-23/6/32.**G.**
Don.22/2-11/4/33.**G.**
Don.16/3-15/5/34.**G.**
Don.26/2-4/4/35.**G.**
Don.7/2-26/3/36.**G.**
Don.29/1-25/3/37.**G.**
Don.31/5-7/7/38.**G.**
Don.26/8-13/10/39.**G.**
Hudd ATC fitted.
Don.25/8-8/10/41.**G.**
Don.28/1-4/2/42.**L.**
Don.6/1-7/2/43.**G.**

Repairs:- **C/H**-Casual Heavy.   **C/L**-Casual Light.   **G**-General.   **H**-Heavy.   **H/I**-Heavy Intermediate.   **L**-Light.   **L/I**-Light Intermediate.   **N/C**-Non-Classified.
Works:-   Cow - Cowlairs.   Dar - Darlington.   Don - Doncaster.   Gat - Gateshead.   Gor - Gorton.   Hay - Haymarket shed.   SRX - St Rollox.

40

2500 was the first of an order for nine which completed the building of class A3. It also introduced the 'banjo' type of steam collecting dome when new on 10th July 1934.

Don.26/11/43-11/1/44.**G.**
Don.21/4-9/6/45.**G.**
Don.11/6-20/7/46.**G.**
Don.20/10-24/11/47.**G.**
Don.3/3-13/4/49.**G.**
Don.9/10-15/11/50.**G.**
Don.6/8-3/9/52.**G.**
Don.15/1-17/2/54.**G.**
Don.9/7-15/8/55.**G.**
Don.3/12/56-16/1/57.**H/I.**
Don.14-20/3/57.**C/L.**
Don.24-30/4/57.**C/L.**
Don.1-22/11/57.**C/L.**
Don.5/8-25/9/58.**G.**
Don.26/8-26/9/59.**C/L.**
Don.8/6-28/7/60.**G.**
Don.24/7-17/8/61.**C/L.**
Don.15/5-13/8/62.**G.**

BOILERS:
8247
8031 (ex2578) 11/4/33
8078 (ex2598) 4/4/35
8076 (ex2580) 25/3/37
8077 (ex2751) 8/10/41
9213 (ex4477) 24/11/47
9117 (ex2572) 13/4/49.
9117 renumbered 27009
15/11/50.
27036 (ex60084) 3/9/52
27066 (ex60079) 17/2/54
27047 (ex60107) 25/9/58
27057 (ex60036) 17/8/61
27063 (ex60106) 13/8/62

TENDERS:
5480 17/5/30-30/6/30
5332 30/6/30-29/1/37
5640 25/3/37-31/5/38
5275 7/7/38-28/1/42
5286 4/2/42-3/3/49

5283 13/4/49-6/8/52
5566 3/9/52-19/6/65

SHEDS:
Haymarket
Aberdeen 4/4/37
Haymarket 6/3/38
Eastfield 19/7/38
Dundee 5/10/40
Haymarket 14/12/40
St Margarets 6/1/63

RENUMBERED:
No.100. 20/7/46
No.60100. 13/4/49

CONDEMNED:
19/6/65.
Into Darlington Works for repair 31/5/65 but condemned and cut-up.

2797
CICERO

Doncaster   1742

To traffic   4/6/30

REPAIRS:
Don.16/9-31/10/31.**G.**
Don.22/11/32-4/1/33.**G.**
Don.24/1-22/3/34.**G.**
Don.18/4-25/5/35.**G.**
Don.29/4-17/6/36.**G.**
Don.24/5-6/7/37.**G.**
Don.10/10-18/11/38.**G.**
Don.11-15/5/39.**L.**
Damaged.
Don.3/11-16/12/39.**G.**

Don.27/6-8/8/41.**G.**
Hudd ATC fitted.
Don.21-28/8/41.**L.**
Don.2-23/9/42.**L.**
Cow.1-3/10/42.**L.**
Don.24/12/42-27/1/43.**G.**
Don.24/5-25/6/44.**G.**
Don.6/9-21/10/45.**G.**
Don.6-15/3/46.**L.**
Don.18-28/9/46.**L.**
Don.16/4-22/5/47.**G.**
Don.9/7-20/8/48.**G.**
Don.31/10-2/12/49.**G.**
Don.13/8-20/9/51.**G.**
Don.16/4-21/5/53.**G.**
Hay.30/12/53-22/1/54.**C/L.**
Hay.22/7-11/8/54.**C/L.**
Don.8/10-16/11/54.**G.**
Don.5/11/55-6/1/56.**H/I.**
Don.17/7-29/8/57.**G.**
Don.5/1-20/2/59.**G.**
Don.28/6-18/8/60.**G.**

BOILERS:
8248
8082 (ex2747) 22/3/34
8223 (ex2599) 25/5/35
8776 (ex2500) 27/1/43
8248 (ex4471) 22/5/47
8080 (ex109) 2/12/49
27057 (ex60060) 20/9/51
29281 (ex60031) 16/11//54
27029 (ex60058) 29/8/57
27083 (ex60042) 20/2/59
27011 (ex60103) 18/8/60

TENDERS:
5481 31/5/30-24/5/37
5571 6/7/37-11/4/63

SHEDS:
Haymarket
Dundee 15/2/37
Eastfield 20/11/38
St Margarets 2/2/40
Haymarket 19/10/40
St Margarets 6/1/63

RENUMBERED:
No.101. 14/7/46
No.60101. 20/8/48

CONDEMNED:
11/4/63.
Sold for scrap to Arnott Young, Carmyle 6/64.

2500
WINDSOR LAD

Doncaster   1790

To traffic   10/7/34

REPAIRS:
Don.19/3-2/5/35.**G.**
Don.7/4-23/5/36.**G.**
Don.22/1-12/3/37.**G.**
Don.14/4-27/5//38.**G.**
Don.16/9-28/10/39.**G.**
Hudd ATC fitted.
Don.22/1-7/3/41.**G.**
Cow.21-27/8/41.**L.**
Cow.1-4/10/41.**L.**
Don.11/3-18/4/42.**G.**
Don.5/7-13/8/43.**G.**
Don.5/1-24/2/45.**G.**
Don.20/5-20/6/46.**G.**
Don.28/7-3/9/47.**G.**
Don.18/10-25/11/48.**G.**

2504 was one of the four which began work from Gateshead shed, the other five of the last batch going new to Haymarket but on 30th November 1935 Southern Area took 2504 in exchange for A4 No.2511, so that Gateshead shed had a streamlined engine in reserve if needed to work *The Silver Jubilee*. 2504 then worked from Doncaster. In September 1937 at that station it is about to leave on an express to Kings Cross and provides proof that a Brownie box camera (the only camera I ever had) could take acceptable railway photos.

Don.30/11/49-13/1/50.**G.**
Don.17/7-16/8/51.**G.**
Don.26/8-6/10/52.**G.**
Don.31/3-7/5/54.**G.**
Hay.18/10-7/11/54.**C/L.**
Don.13/9-20/10/55.**G.**
Don.27/4-19/6/57.**G.**
Dar.5-13/5/58.**C/L.**
Don.3/12/58-21/9/59.**G.**
Don.21/4-31/5/60.**G.**

BOILERS:
8776
9121 (New) 7/3/41
8084 (ex2576) 25/11/48
27053 (ex60085) 16/8/51
27048 (ex60085) 7/5/54
27070 (ex60110) 19/6/57
27058 (ex60052) 21/1/59
27001 (ex60102) 31/5/60

TENDERS:
5567 16/6/34-4/9/61

SHEDS:
Haymarket
Aberdeen 28/3/37
Haymarket 4/4/37
Carlisle Canal 23/4/61
Haymarket 28/8/61

RENUMBERED:
No.570. 7/4/46
No.35. 15/6/46
No.60035. 25/11/48

CONDEMNED:
4/9/61, after entering Doncaster Works for repair 26/8/61. Cut-up Doncaster.

2501
COLOMBO

Doncaster   1791

To traffic   9/7/34

REPAIRS:
Don.12/4-15/5/35.**G.**
Dar.19/8-1/9/35.**N/C.** *Lifted for Left Trailing hot box.*
Don.31/1-6/3/36.**G.**
Don.20/2-3/4/37.**G.**
Dar.8-15/4/37.**N/C.**
Left Leading bearing hot.
Don.3/3-8/4/38.**G.**
Don.10-14/11/38.**L**
Don.5-13/6/39.**G.**
Don.25/11/40-4/1/41.**G.**
Don.7/2-29/7/42.**G.**

Don.10-16/10/42.**L.**
Fitted with indicator box.
Don.8/2-18/3/44.**G.**
Don.5/5-23/6/45.**G.**
Don.1/3-12/4/47.**G.**
Don.7-18/6/47.**L.**
Collision at Peterborough.
Dar.15/10/47.**N/C.**
Don.29/5-23/7/48.**G.**
Don.8/6-22/7/49.**G.**
Don.17/11-20/12/50.**G.**
Don.9/11-18/12/51.**G.**
Don.26/11-9/12/52.**G.**
Don.29/1-14/2/53.**L.**
Don.21/7-25/8/53.**G.**
Don.13-29/4/54.**C/L.**
Don.1/11-8/12/54.**G.**
Don.18/2-6/4/56.**G.**
Don.30/9-9/11/57.**G.**
Don.12-23/7/58.**N/C.**
Don.29/8-14/11/58.**G.**
York buffer stop collision.
Don.2-4/3/59.**N/C.**
Don.11-19/6/59.**N/C.**
Don.11-17/9/59.**N/C.**
Don.9/5-29/6/60.**G.**
Don.24/5-19/7/62.**G.**

BOILERS:
8777

9124 (New) 4/1/41
9568 (New) 12/4/47
9511 (ex2504) 23/7/48
9980 (New) 22/7/49. *9980 renumbered 27021 20/12/50.*
27064 (ex60054) 18/12/51
27059 (ex60067) 25/8/53
27039 (ex60109) 8/12/54
27078 (ex60050) 6/4/56
27057 (ex60039) 9/11/57
29328 (ex60023) 29/6/60
29308 (ex60054) 19/7/62

TENDERS:
5568 30/6/34-9/2/44
5227 17/3/44-23/11/64

SHEDS:
Gateshead
York 9/12/39
Heaton 28/3/43
Gateshead 3/11/45
Kings Cross 1/8/47
Gateshead 9/9/47
Neville Hill 6/2/49
Copley Hill 11/6/61
Ardsley 10/9/61
Gateshead 16/6/63
Darlington 15/12//63

Repairs:- **C/H**-Casual Heavy. **C/L**-Casual Light. **G**-General. **H**-Heavy. **H/I**-Heavy Intermediate. **L**-Light. **L/I**-Light Intermediate. **N/C**-Non-Classified.
Works:- **Cow** - Cowlairs. **Dar** - Darlington. **Don** - Doncaster. **Gat** - Gateshead. **Gor** - Gorton. **Hay** - Haymarket shed. **SRX** - St Rollox.

RENUMBERED:
No.36. 1/12/46
No.60036. 23/7/48

CONDEMNED:
23/11/64.
Sold for scrap to A. Draper,
Hull 1/65.

2502
HYPERION

Doncaster   1792

To traffic   25/7/34

REPAIRS:
Don.28/1-7/2/35.**L.**
Don.20/6-19/7/35.**G.**
Don.3-21/12/35.**L.**
After collision.
Don.6/8-24/9/36.**G.**
Don.11/10-13/11/37.**G.**
Don.22/9-14/10/38.**L.**
Don.27/1-8/3/39.**G.**
Don.26/1-15/3/40.**G.**
Don.27/6-15/8/41.**G.**
Don.22/12/42-30/1/43.**G.**
Don.28/7-26/8/44.**G.**
Don.31/8-8/9/44.**L.**
Don.18/2-30/3/46.**G**
Don.4/6-12/7/47.**G.**
Don.15/9-27/10/48.**G.**
Don.9/5-22/6/50.**G.**
Don.14/2-19/3/52.**G.**
Don.1/10-10/11/53.**G.**
Don.28/11-21/12/53.**N/C.**
Don.25/3-22/4/54.**C/L.**
Hay.22/7-10/8/54.**C/L.**
Don.24/6-5/8/55.**G.**
Don.25/5-23/6/56.**C/L.**
Cow.14-16/2/57.**N/C.**
Don.11/3-18/4/57.**G.**
Don.29-4-9/5/57.**C/L.**
Don.21/8-8/10/58.**G.**
Don.25/8-26/9/59.**C/L**
Don.26/10-6/11/59.**C/L.**
Don.18/5-15/7/60.**G.**
Don.23/3-19/5/62.**G.**
Don.21/5-19/7/63.**C/L**

BOILERS:
8778
  8777 (ex2501) 15/8/41
  8720 (ex2595) 12/7/47
  10541 (new) 22/6/50. *10541*
  renumbered 27072 19/3/52.
  27068 (ex60108) 10/11/53
  27027 (ex60087) 18/4/57
  27066 (ex60100) 8/10/58
  27058 (ex60035) 15/7/60
  27004 (ex60075) 19/5/62

TENDERS:
5570 14/7/34-27/6/41
5261 15/8/41-9/5/50
5285 22/6/50-4/5/57
5276 9/5/57-12/12/63

SHEDS:
Haymarket
St Margarets 6/3/38
Haymarket 15/3/39
Carlisle 7/2/54

Haymarket 8/3/54
St Margarets 6/11/61

RENUMBERED:
No.37. 25/8/46
No.60037. 25/10/48

CONDEMNED:
12/12/63.
Sold for scrap to Arnott,
Young. Carmyle 6/64.

2503
FIRDAUSSI

Doncaster   1793

To traffic   11/8/34

REPAIRS:
Don.6/6-16/7/35.**G.**
Don.4/6-9/7/36.**G.**
Don.14-18/12/36.**L.**
Don.21/5-24/6/37.**G.**
Don.3/5-25/6/38.**G.**
Don.14-29/7/38.**L.**
Don.27/3-27/4/39.**G.**
Don.18-25/4/40.**G.**
Don.17/9-2/11/40.**H.**
Don.16/2-2/4/42.**G.**
Don.8-25/9/42.**L.**
Don.9/9-19/10/43.**G.**
Don.16/3-1/4/44.**L.**
Don.12/7-21/9/45.**G.**
Don.23/1-13/3/47.**G.**
Don.30/7-22/9/48.**G.**
Don.12/12/49-20/1/50.**G.**
Don.9/8-6/9/51.**H/I.**
Don.29/12/52-29/1/53.**G.**
Don.13/12/54-20/1/55.**G.**
Don.15-22/3/55.**N/C.**
Don.15/5-19/6/56.**G.**
Gat.30/10-20/11/57.**C/L.**
Don.7/3-18/4/58.**G.**
Don.19/3-9/4/59.**C/L.**
Don.11/8-30/9/59.**G.**
Don.19/4-2/6/61.**G.**

BOILERS:
8779
  8075 (ex2750) 19/10/43
  9512 (ex2743) 22/9/48
  9116 (ex42) 20/1/50. *9116*
  renumbered 27058 6/9/51.
  27038 (ex60066) 29/1/53
  27040 (ex60074) 20/1/55
  27018 (ex60098) 18/4/58
  27003 (ex60041) 30/9/59
  27960 (ex60020) 2/6/61

TENDERS:
5571 11/8/34-21/5/37
5583 24/6/37-18/11/63

SHEDS:
Gateshead
Heaton 30/9/39/
  Gateshead 10/11/39
Heaton 4/1/43
Gateshead 3/5/43
Darlington 22/2/53
Gateshead 30/8/53
Darlington 19/8/56
Gateshead 24/2/57

Holbeck 21/2/60
Neville Hill 16/6/63

RENUMBERED:
No.38 27/10/46
No.60038 10/6/48

CONDEMNED:
18/11/63.
Into Darlington Works for
cut-up 31/12/63.

2504
SANDWICH

Doncaster   1794

To traffic   9/9/34

REPAIRS:
Don.11/10-22/11/35.**G.**
Don.2/12/36-15/1/37.**G.**
Don.17-19/11/37.**L.**
Blowdown apparatus fitted.
Don.28/1-8/3/38.**G.**
Don.8-9/4/38.**L.**
Don.30/3-11/5/39.**H.**
Don.28/2-12/3/40.**L.**
Don.29/5-22/6/40.**G.**
Don.5-26/8/41.**L.**
Don.6-17/10/41.**L.**
Don.8/8-25/9/42.**G.**
Don.9-16/2/43.**L.**
Don.17-30/9/43.**L.**
Don.11-18/11/43.**L.**
Don.3/4-4/5/44.**G.**
Don.10/4-2/6/45.**G.**
Don.13/10-1/11/45.**L.**
Don.16/7-7/9/46.**G.**
Don.28/5-9/7/48.**G.**
Don.23/1-31/3/50.**G.**
Don.12-17/4/50.**N/C.**
Don.17-24/10/50.**C/L.**
Don.21/9-26/10/51.**G.**
Don.19-27/5/52.**C/L.**
Don.10/2-11/3/53.**G.**
Don.20-29/1/54.**N/C.**
Don.31/1-4/3/55.**G.**
Don.9/5-5/7/56.**G.**
Don.24/8-5/10/57.**G.**
Don.12-28/12/57.**C/L.**
After collision.
Don.19/12/58-10/1/59.**C/L.**
Don.12/6-31/7/59.**G.**
Don.9/3/60.**N/C.**
Don.19/7-16/8/60.**C/L.**
Don.12/4-2/6/61.**G.**
Don.12/2-3/3/62.**C/L.**
Don.5-27/7/62.**C/L.**
Don.17/9-31/10/62.**C/L.**

BOILERS:
8780
  9115 (New) 11/5/39
  9511 (New) 7/9/46
  9208 (ex2574) 9/7/48
  9512 (ex38) 31/3/50
  27060 (ex60035) 26/10/51
  27022 (ex60064) 11/3/53
  27057 (ex60101) 4/3/55
  27014 (ex60091) 5/10/57
  29294 (ex60063) 31/7/59
  27968 (New) 2/6/61

TENDERS:
5573 8/9/34-14/3/63

SHEDS:
Gateshead
Doncaster 30/11/35
Kings Cross 6/3/39
Grantham 9/12/41
Kings Cross 4/6/50
Grantham 9/9/51
Leicester Cen. 7/10/56
Kings Cross 7/4/57

RENUMBERED:
No.39. 8/7/46
No.60039. 9/7/48

CONDEMNED:
14/3/63.
Into Doncaster Works for
cut-up 5/4/63.

2505
CAMERONIAN

Doncaster   1795

To traffic   27/10/34

REPAIRS:
Don.5-15/3/35.**L.**
Don.6-24/5/35.**L.**
Don.15/10-23//11/35.**G.**
Don.6/10-13/11/36.**G.**
Don.12/10-13/11/37.**G.**
Don.19/10-26/11/38.**G.**
Dar.8-23/5/39.
For test purposes.
Don.13/12/39-20/1/40.**G.**
Don.24/12/40-/30/1/41.**G.**
Don.24/4-9/5/41.**H.**
Don.27/10-29/11/42.**G.**
Don.28/5-17/6/43.**L.**
Don.21/3-27/4/44.**H.**
Don.2/7-2/9/45.**G.**
Don.11-27/4/46.**L.**
Don.11/2-22/3/47.**G.**
Don.9/7-31/8/48.**G.**
Don.24/10-1/12/49.**G.**
Don.19/12/50-24/1/51.**H/I.**
Don.24/4-23/5/52.**G.**
Don.18/7-18/8/53.**G.**
Gat.9-16/7/54.**N/C.**
Gat.17-25/2/55.**N/C.**
Don.20/5-14/7/55.**G.**
Gat.3-14/7/56.**C/L.**
Don.6/9-4/10/56.**C/L.**
Don.16/8-4/10/57.**G.**
Don.19-26/10/57.**N/C.**
Don.25/9-4/10/58.**N/C.**
Don.1/9-16/10/59.**G.**
Don.16/3-28/4/61.**C/L.**
Don.12/2-24/3/62.**G.**
Dar.6-19/12/63.**N/C.**

BOILERS:
8781
  9116 (New) 20/1/40
  9119 (New) 9/5/41
  9445 (ex4478) 22/3/47
  9447 (ex50) 1/12/49. *9447*
  renumbered 27026 24/1/51.
  27001 (ex60078) 23/5/52
  27035 (ex60088) 18/8/53

2506 began with a high-sided tender, and had a corridor type from 17th October 1935 until 7th December 1936 but was never called upon to run the non-stop *Flying Scotsman.* **It then, as here in July 1939, had the first of a couple of railed tenders to withdrawal.**

27077 (ex60108) 14/7/55
27079 (ex60097) 4/10/57
27018 (ex60038) 16/10/59
27012 (ex60061) 24/3/62

TENDERS:
5566 24/10/34-13/11/36
5253 13/11/36-4/7/64

SHEDS:
Haymarket
Gateshead 16/11/36
York 2/12/39
Gateshead 9/12/39
Heaton 28/3/43
Gateshead 3/11/45
Darlington 20/9/53
Gateshead 21/3/54
Darlington 7/8/55
Gateshead 12/2/56
Darlington 3/11/57
Gateshead 4/5/58
Darlington 6/12/59
Gateshead 19/6/60
Darlington 24/6/62
Heaton 9/12/62
Gateshead 16/6/63

RENUMBERED:
No.575. 17/3/46
No.40. 19/5/46
No.60040. 31/8/48

CONDEMNED:
6/7/64
Sold for scrap to Hughes
Bolckow, North Blyth 9/64.

2506
SALMON TROUT

Doncaster   1797

To traffic   19/12/34

REPAIRS:
Don.24/10-3/12/35.**G.**
Don.7/12/36-30/1/37.**G.**
Don.28/1-11/3/38.**G.**
Don.10/5-8/7/39.**G.**
Hudd ATC Fitted.
Cow.4-5/5/40.**L.**
Don.27/11-40-10/1/41.**G.**
Don.3/4-9/5/42.**G.**
Don.6/10-4/11/43.**G.**
Don.30/10-9/12/44.**G.**
Don.17-28/10/45.**L.**
Don.19/11-29/12/45.**G.**
Don.24/3-7/5/47.**G.**
Don.19/10-26/11/48.**G.**
Don.26/5-7/7/50.**G.**
Don.18-20/7/50.**N/C.**
Don.16/1-13/2/52.**G.**
Don.28/4-28/5/53.**G.**
Don.16/12/54-26/1/55.**G.**
Don.21/4-3/5/55.**C/L.**
Don.4/9-24/10/56.**G.**
Don.13-22/3/57.**C//L.**
Don.15/1-20/2/58.**G.**
Don.17/6-31/7/59.**G.**
Don.18/9-1/10/59.**N/C.**
Don.11/2/61-23/3/61.**G.**
Cow.31/5-7/6/61.**N/C.**
Don.10/12/62-17/1/63.**G.**

BOILERS:
8782
8780 (ex2504) 10/1/41
9482 (New) 29/12/45
9118 (ex94) 7/7/50
27067 (ex60043) 13/2/52
27082 (ex60098) 24/10/56
27003 (ex60092) 20/2/58
27049 (ex60098) 31/7/59
27020 (ex60110) 23/3/61
27024 (ex60045) 17/1/63

TENDERS:
5581 19/12/34-17/10/35

5325 17/10/35-7/12/36
5226 30/1/37-30/10/44
5272 9/12/44-4/12/65

SHEDS:
Haymarket
St Margarets 13/7/60

RENUMBERED:
No.41. 7/7/46
No.60041. 26/11/48

CONDEMNED:
4/12/65.
Sold for scrap to Arnott
Young, Carmyle 9/66.

2507
SINGAPORE

Doncaster   1798

To traffic   1/12/34

REPAIRS:
Don.19/12/35-29/1/36.**G.**
Don.7/1-20/2/37.**G.**
Don.13/10-19/11/37.**G.**
Don.21/11/38-6/1/39.**G.**
Don.21/1-3/2/40.**G.**
Don.7/7-5/9/41.**G.**
Don.9/9-1/10/42.**L.**
Don.20/7-25/8/43.**G.**
Don.2-12/9/43.**N/C.**
Don.18/1-3/3/45.**G.**
Don.27/11/46-4/1/47.**G.**
Don.14/6-12/8/48.**G.**
Don.15/11-16/12/49.**G.**
Don.19/4-17/5/51.**G.**
Don.11/11-18/12/52.**G.**
Don.18/10-4/11/54.**C/L.**
Don.29/3-4/5/55.**G.**
Don.30/7-8/9/56.**G.**

Don.30/7-5/9/58.**G.**
Don.29/3-6/5/60.**G.**
Don.8/6-5/9/62.**G.**

BOILERS:
8783
8782 (ex2506) 5/9/41
9116 (ex109) 12/8/48
9214 (ex4480) 16/12/49
27046 (ex60086) 17/5/51
27076 (ex60094) 4/5/55
27083 (ex60107) 8//9/56
27024 (ex60054) 5/9/58
27002 (ex60106) 6/5/60

TENDERS:
5582 1/12/34-7/1/37
5639 20/2/37-13/10/37
5229 19/11/37-7/7/41
5570 5/9/41-20/7/43
5274 25/8/43-11/11/52
5260 17/12/52-13/7/64

SHEDS:
Gateshead
Neville Hill 27/9/45
Gateshead 6/5/46
Darlington 22/3/53
Gateshead 20/9/53
Darlington 7/3/54
Gateshead 5/9/54
Darlington 11/11/56
Gateshead 5/5/57
Heaton 9/9/62
Aberdeen 7/4/63
St Margarets 27/10/63

RENUMBERED:
No.42. 10/11/46
No.60042. 9/4/48

CONDEMNED:
13/7/64.

Repairs:- C/H-Casual Heavy. C/L-Casual Light. G-General. H-Heavy. H/I-Heavy Intermediate. L-Light. L/I-Light Intermediate. N/C-Non-Classified.
Works:- Cow - Cowlairs. Dar - Darlington. Don - Doncaster. Gat - Gateshead. Gor - Gorton. Hay - Haymarket shed. SRX - St Rollox.

Sold for scrap to Arnott Young, Carmyle 10/64.

2508
BROWN JACK

Doncaster   1800

To traffic   9/2/35

REPAIRS:
Don.12/2-28/3/36.**G.**
Don.9/2-2/4/37.**G.**
Don.19/4-21/5/38.**G.**
Don.19/8-6/10/39.**G.**
Hudd ATC Fitted.
Don.27/12/40-7/2/41.**G.**
Don.2/5-8/6/42.**G.**
Don.8/12/43-8/1/44.**G.**
Don.11/7-8/9/45.**G.**
Don.8-23/8/46.**G.**
Don.5/5-8/6/47.**G.**
Don.21/6-11/8/48.**G.**
Don.14/3-21/4/50.**G.**
Don.27/4-2/5/50.**N/C.**
Don.24/7-24/8/51.**G.**
Don.17/12/52-22/1/53.**G.**
Hay.12/2-6/3/54.**L/I.**
Don.2/4-25/5/54.**H/I.**
Don.5/10-23/11/55.**G.**
Don.19/9-23/10//56.**C/L.**
Don.18/1-6/2/57.**N/C.**
Don.2/7-21/8/57.**G.**
Don.25/12/58-21/2/59.**G.**
Don.27/6-5/8/60.**G.**
Don.20/12/61-3/2/62.**G.**
Cow.16/10-6/12/62.**N/C.**

Only one of the twenty seven built as A3s acquired the E prefix to the number which British Railways used from mid-January 1948, only a couple of months before the 60000 numbering was introduced. E99 ran as such from 5th March 1948 until it went into works on 8th June 1949, coming out on 21st July as 60099.

BOILERS:
8784
8781 (ex2505) 7/2/41
9447 (New) 8/1/44
9570 (ex67) 11/8/48
9212 (ex105) 21/4/50
27055 (ex60105) 24/8/51
27075 (ex60073) 23/11/55
27021 (ex60062) 21/8/57
27011 (ex60103) 21/2/59
29339 (New) 5/8/60
29285 (ex60102) 3/2/62

TENDERS:
5584 9/2/35-5/4/35
5330 5/4/35-9/2/37
5641 2/4/37-19/4/38
5256 21/5/38-14/5/64

SHEDS:
Haymarket
St Margarets 6/11/61

RENUMBERED:
No.43. 23/8/46
No.60043. 11/8/48

CONDEMNED:
14/5/64.
Sold for scrap to Motherwell Machinery & Scrap Co. Inshaw 7/64.

2507 worked its first eleven years from Gateshead shed, and is seen in 1939 passing through Doncaster station on the up main line. The railed tender, which served it from 19th November 1937 until 7th July 1941, had originally started work with A1 No.4478.

2508 was always shedded in Edinburgh and in the summers of 1935 and 1936 established a high reputation for consecutive trips on the non-stop workings, before its corridor tender was taken by A4 No.4487.

Re-numbering began in 1946 and No.2573 changed to 542 on 7th April. A further nineteen engines got numbers in the 500 series before a revised instruction at the end of April allocated numbers 35 to 112 for the A3 (and remaining A10) class. 517 on the 25th April was the last in that series.

Pending a decision, LNER green livery continued to be applied until the end of April 1949. Ex works on 13th May, Nos.60086 and 60102 appeared in blue of a different shade to those done in 1948, and were lined in black and white. There was also a change from BRITISH RAILWAYS to the lion and wheel emblem.

60100 duly acquired all the latest fittings put on A3s. Its final repair was in August 1962, though trough deflectors were fitted at a light repair in August 1961. Before returning to its home shed in Edinburgh, Doncaster used it to work south, and here at Grantham it shows every indication it is bound for London.

In April 1927 Doncaster works were given an order to build five new boilers for Pacifics, two for spares in the Southern Area and three for spares in the North Eastern Area. The opportunity was taken to increase the pressure from 180 to 220 lb and also to up-rate the superheater from 32 to 43 elements. It was calculated this would make the locos 22% more powerful. The first of these boilers was put into No.4480 *ENTERPRISE* which went back to traffic on 15th July 1927 and was re-classified to A3. At the same rebuilding, it was given longer valve travel.

No.2544 *LEMBERG* was the other Southern Area engine rebuilt to A3 class and was ex works on 3rd December 1927. This view shows it as ex works on 16th April 1932 after fitting with automatic blow-down valve.

The other three higher pressure boilers were sent to Darlington in December 1927, January 1928, and on 25th March 1928; the engines to get them were 2580 (16th February 1928), 2573 (17th April 1928) and, 2578 (22nd May 1928). The first two very soon acquired corridor tender and took part in the early runs of the non-stop *Flying Scotsman* , working from the Edinburgh end. 2578 only ever had one change of tender, in March 1938, and kept the railed type throughout. Here on 28th July 1934 it is about to leave Newcastle for Edinburgh on the *Queen of Scots Pullman*.

PART THREE

THE A1/A10 REBUILT TO CLASS A3

Repairs:-	**C/H**-Casual Heavy.	**C/L**-Casual Light.	**G**-General.	**H**-Heavy.	**H/I**-Heavy Intermediate. **L**-Light. **L/I**-Light Intermediate. **N/C**-Non-Classified.
Works:-	Cow - Cowlairs.	Dar - Darlington.	Don - Doncaster.	Gat - Gateshead.	Gor - Gorton. Hay - Haymarket shed. SRX - St Rollox.

44
MELTON

Rebuilt Doncaster from A10

To traffic   18/9/47

REPAIRS:
Don.6/7-11/8/49.**G.**
Don.22-30/8/50.**L.**
Don.5/2-8/3/51.**G.**
Don.22/1-1/2/52.**N/C.**
Don.12/11-4/12/52.**H/I.**
Don.15/3-26/4/54.**C/L.**
Don.21/11-31/12/54.**G.**
Don.3-27/4/56.**C/L.**
Don.4-10/5/56.**N/C.**
Don.29/10-6/12/56.**G.**
Don.28/3-7/5/58.**G.**
Don.1-10/6/59.**N/C.**
Don.15/9-21/10/59.**G.**
Don.29/2-11/3/60.**C/L.**
Don.5/10-5/11/60.**C/L.**
Don.12-30/8/61.**G.**
Don.3-21/4/62.**C/L.**
Don.28/8-28/9/62.**C/L.**
Don.18/2-12/3/63.**C/L.**

BOILERS:
 8226 (ex2566)
 9984 (New) 11/8/49
27033 (ex60099) 8/3/51
27039 (ex60036) 6/12/56
27035 (ex60104) 7/5/58
27072 (ex60089) 21/10/59

TENDERS:
5580 -12/11/52
5274 18/12/52-16/6/63

SHEDS:
New England
Grantham 9/11/47
Copley Hill 23/4/50
Doncaster 9/9/51
Leicester Cen 15/11/53
Neasden 27/3/55
Kings Cross 25/3/56
Grantham 16/9/56
Kings Cross 7/4/57

RENUMBERED:
No.60044. 11/8/49

CONDEMNED:
16/6/63.
Into Doncaster Works
for cut-up 25/11/63.

2544
LEMBERG

Rebuilt Doncaster from A1

To traffic   3/12/27

REPAIRS:
Don.17-19/1/28.**N/C.**
Don.20-24/1/28.**L.**
Don.6-9/2/28.**L.**
Don.12/7-16/8/28.**H.**
Don.21/12/28-8/4/29.**G.**
Don.3/9-12/10/29.**H.**
Don.18/12/30-31/1/31.**G.**
Don.2-5/3/31.**N/C.**
Don.17/2-16/4/32.**G.**
Don.13-17/6/32.**L.**
Don.2/3-4/5/33.**H.**
Don.5/12/34-18/1/35.**G.**
Don.8-15/8/35.**L.**
Don.13-16/11/35.**L.**
Don.28/3-14/5/36.**G.**
Don.8/4-14/5/37.**G.**
Don.22/2-26/3/38.**G.**
Don.10/5/38.**L.**
Don.1/5-13/6/39.**G.**
Don.20/3-11/4/40.**L.**
Don.16/9-26/10/40.**G.**
Don.23/6-5/7/41.**L.**
Don.8/4-20/5/42.**G.**
Don.26-28/5/42.**N/C.**
Don.30/7-16/9/43.**G.**
Don.14/2-11/3/44.**L.**
Don.21/8-8/9/44.**L.**
Don.16/10-28/11/45.**G.**
Don.31/8-28/9/46.**L.**
Don.16/5-18/6/47.**G.**
Don.24/5-5/6/48.**L.**
Don.13/1-26/2/49.**G.**
Dar.13/12/49-19/1/50.**C/L.**
Don.2/10-8/11/50.**G.**
Don.17/3-18/4/52.**G.**
Don.9-27/10/52.**L.**
Don.22/9-28/10/53.**G.**
Don.3/10-3/11/55.**G.**
Don.22/7-2/8/57.**C/L.**
Don.4/12/57-17/1/58.**G.**
Don.14-22/4/58.**N/C.**
Don.28/9-17/10/59.**C/L.**
Don.4-24/12/59.**C/L.**
Don.13/2-5/3/60.**C/L.**
Don.2/4-3/6/60.**G.**
Don.28/8-1/11/62.**G.**

BOILERS:
 8028 (new)
 8027 (ex4480) 31/1/31
 8224 (ex2596) 4/5/33
 8029 (ex2744) 14/5/36
 8226 (ex2578) 14/5/37
 8248 (ex4480) 26/3/38
 8031 (ex2752) 20/5/42
 8250 (ex2599) 18/6/47
 9450 (ex2749) 26/2/49

Rebuilt Doncaster from A1

To traffic   3/12/27

27007 (New) 8/11/50
27063 (ex60055) 28/10/53
27028 (ex60078) 17/1/58
27024 (ex60042) 3/6/60
27021 (ex60062) 1/11/62

TENDERS:
5254 -21/12/28
5228 8/4/29-23/11/64

SHEDS:
Doncaster
Gateshead 6/1/37
Heaton 17/5/38
Gateshead 22/1/40
Darlington 28/2/54
Gateshead 7/3/54
Darlington 21/3/54
Gateshead 26/10/54
Darlington 13/11/55
Gateshead 27/5/56
Darlington 4/5/58
Gateshead 16/11/58
Heaton 9/9/62
Darlington 9/12/62
Heaton 2/6/63
Gateshead 16/6/63
Darlington 15/12/63

RENUMBERED:
No.45. 3/11/46
No.60045. 4/6/48

CONDEMNED:
23/11/64.
Sold to A.Draper,
Hull for scrap 1/65

2545
DIAMOND JUBILEE

Rebuilt Doncaster from A1

To traffic   23/8/41

REPAIRS:
Don.10/2-14/3/43.**G.**
Don.7/4-29/5/45.**G.**
Don.27/5-13/7/46.**G.**
Don.28/10-15/11/46.**L.**
Don.2/10-13/11/47.**G.**
Don.5/6-5/8/49.**G.**
Don.18-22/9/50.**C/L.**
Don.29/4-1/6/51.**G.**
Don.23/9-29/10/52.**H/I.**
Don.21/7-20/8/54.**G.**
Don.23-30/8/54.**N/C.**
Don.7-8/2/55.*Weigh.*
Don.3/11-21/12/56.**G.**
Don.3/7-8/8/58.**G.**

Don.1/12/59-6/1/60.**G.**
Don.30/8-29/9/60.**C/L.**
Don.17/1-4/2/61.**C/L.**
Don.20/10-7/12/61.**G.**
Don.29/10-22/11/62.**C/L.**

BOILERS:
 9122 (New)
 9510 (New) 13/7/46
 9983 (New) 5/8/49
27047 (ex60112) 1/6/51
27051 (ex60105) 20/8/54
27069 (ex60080) 8/8/58
29306 (ex60099) 6/1/60
27086 (ex60089) 7/12/61

TENDERS:
5644 -16/6/63

SHEDS:
Grantham
Copley Hill 30/9/43
Kings Cross 8/12/44
Copley Hill 30/5/48
Doncaster 9/9/51
Grantham 14/6/59
New England 9/9/62
Grantham 21/4/63

RENUMBERED:
No.46. 13/7/46
No.60046. 5/8/49

CONDEMNED:
16/6/63.
Into Doncaster works
for cut-up 20/8/63.

47
DONOVAN

Rebuilt Doncaster from A10

To traffic   9/1/48 *

REPAIRS:
Don.28/4-8/5/48.**L.**
Don.1/5-16/6/49.**G.**
Don.24-31/8/49.**C/L.**
Don.23/10-6/12/50.**G.**
Don.13/1-20/2/52.**G.**
Don.9-15/2/53.**N/C.**
Don.15/6-27/7/53.**G.**
Don.8/9-26/10/54.**G.**
Don.22/12/55-25/1/56.**C/L.**
Don.2/5-18/7/56.**G.**
Don.12/11-13/12/57.**G.**
Don.17-18/12/57.**N/C.**
Don.21/5-2/7/59.**G.**
Don.22/10-7/11/59.**C/L.**

Don.26/4-19/5/60.**C/L.**
Don.22/11-17/12/60.**C/L.**
Don.13/3-25/4/61.**G.**
Don.8/1-6/2/62.**C/L.**
Don.15/10-9/11/62.**C/L.**

BOILERS:
 8778 (ex2579)
27015 (ex60074) 6/12/50
27069 (ex60081) 20/2/52
27043 (ex60107) 27/7/53
27073 (ex60059) 13/12/57
27042 (ex60060) 2/7/59

TENDERS:
5284 -3/5/48
5280 7/5/48-8/4/63

SHEDS:
Kings Cross
Doncaster 4/6/50
Kings Cross 7/1/51
Grantham 9/9/51
Kings Cross 20/6/54
Grantham 17/10/54
New England 9/9/62

RENUMBERED:
No.60047. 8/5/48

CONDEMNED:
8/4/63.
Into Doncaster works
19/6/63 for cut-up.

** Loco was actually finished
rebuilding 20/12/47 but did
not enter traffic until 9/1/48.*

2547
DONCASTER

Rebuilt Doncaster from A10

To traffic   16/5/46

REPAIRS:
Don.16/5-23/6/47.**G.**
Don.2/10-11/11/48.**G.**
Don.6/8-15/9/50.**G.**
Don.7/8-19/9/52.**G.**
Don.17/1-19/2/53.**N/C.**
Don.11/8-21/9/54.**G.**
Don.28/4-24/5/55.**C/L.**
Don.4/7-17/8/56.**G.**
Don.28/3-17/4/57.**C/L.**
Don.3-26/10/57.**C/L.**
Don.12/3-9/5/58.**G.**
Don.5-10/2/59.**N/C.**
Don.19-29/5/59.**N/C.**
Don.26/10-26/11/59.**G.**
Don.30/5-2/7/60.**C/L.**
Don.28/2-18/3/61.**C/L.**
Don.15/11-15/12/61.**C/L.**
Don.6/3-14/4/62.**G.**
Don.14/1-15/2/63.**C/L.**

BOILERS:
 9123 (ex4473)
 9573 (New) 23/6/47
 9211 (ex65) 11/11/48
10542 (New) 15/9/50
27018 (ex60059) 19/9/52

27047 (ex60046) 21/9/54
27061 (ex60074) 17/8/56
27039 (ex60107) 26/11/59
27083 (ex60108) 14/4/62

TENDERS:
5566 -7/8/52
5283 19/9/52-6/3/62
5483 14/4/62-8/9/63

SHEDS:
Doncaster
Leicester Cen 6/2/49
Doncaster 15/11/53
Kings Cross 8/6/58
Doncaster 25/1/59
Grantham 8/2/59
New England 9/9/62
Grantham 21/4/63

RENUMBERED:
No.48. 16/5/46
No.60048. 11/11/48

CONDEMNED:
8/9/63.
Into Doncaster Works
for cut-up 19/9/63.

2548
GALTEE MORE

Rebuilt Doncaster from A10

To traffic   13/10/45

REPAIRS:
Don.19/2-1/3/46.**L.**
Don.3/11-28/12/46.**G.**
Don.17/5-24/6/48.**G.**
Don.25/7-31/8/50.**G.**
Don.22/8-6/9/51.**C/L.**
Don.10/6-25/7/52.**G.**
Don.4/4-14/5/54.**G.**
Don.10/12/54-13/1/55.**C/L.**
Don.1/11-9/12/55.**G.**
Don.28/6-30/7/56.**C/L**
Don.24/7-17/9/57.**H/I.**
Don.1-7/3/58.**N/C.**
Don.20/10/58.**N/C.**
Don.21/1-4/3/59.**N/C.**
Don.30/10-12/11/59.**N/C.**
Don.15/9-21/10/60.**G.**
Don.6-30/6/61.**C/L.**
Don.5-28/3/62.**C/L.**

BOILERS:
 8224 (exSpare)
 8782 (ex71) 31/8/50
27025 (ex60099) 25/7/52
27053 (ex60035) 14/5/54
27016 (ex60083) 9/12/55
27007 (ex60062) 4/3/59
27005 (ex60062) 21/10/60

TENDERS:
5262 -15/9/60
5232 21/10/60-29/12/62

SHEDS:
Doncaster
Leicester Cen. 6/2/49
Kings Cross 26/6/55
Leicester Cen. 23/10/55

Grantham 15/9/57

RENUMBERED:
No.517. 25/4/46
No.49. 14/7/46
No.60049. 24/6/48

CONDEMNED:
29/12/62.
Into Doncaster Works
for cut-up 4/4/63.

2549
PERSIMMON

Rebuilt Doncaster from A1

To traffic   15/12/43

REPAIRS:
Don.5/7-13/9/45.**G.**
Don.9/2-3/4/47.**G.**
Don.17/1-3/2/48.**L.**
Don.22/6-18/8/48.**G.**
Don.13-27/10/48.**L.**
Don.29/5-27/7/49.**G.**
Don.7/4-4/5/51.**G.**
Don.21/8-26/9/52.**G.**
Don.13/4-8/5/53.**C/L.**
Don.2/7-5/8/54.**G.**
Don.23/9-15/10/54.**C/L.**
Don.26/1-8/3/56.**G.**
Don.23/8-21/9/56.**C/L.**
Don.22/10-29/11/57.**G.**
Don.10-15/3/58.**N/C.**
Don.8-24/10/58.**C/L.**
Don.7-20/4/59.**N/C.**
Don.6-17/6/59.**N/C.**
Don.28/8-15/10/59.**G.**
Don.10/5-2/6/60.**C/L.**
Don.13-31/12/60.**C/L.**
Don.15/8-19/10/61.**G.**
Don.31/8-29/9/62.**C/L.**

BOILERS:
 9446 (New)
 9115 (ex2504) 3/4/47
 9447 (ex2508) 18/8/48
 9122 (ex64) 27/7/49
27045 (ex60044) 4/5/51
27081 (ex60049) 26/9/52
27078 (ex60056) 5/8/54
27084 (ex60088) 8/3/56
27013 (ex60094) 29/11/57
29272 (ex60010) 15/10/59
29299 (ex60095) 19/10/61

TENDERS:
5259 -11/6/63

SHEDS:
Grantham
Kings Cross 27/10/46
Grantham 30/5/48
Kings Cross 16/6/48
Neasden 3/2/49
Kings Cross 3/7/55
Neasden 9/10/55
Kings Cross 24/6/56
Grantham 16/9/56
New England 17/6/62

RENUMBERED:
No.518. 18/3/46

No.50. 8/7/46
No.E50. 3/2/48
No.60050. 18/8/48

CONDEMNED:
11/6/63.
Into Doncaster Works
for cut-up 9/8/63.

2550
BLINK BONNY

Rebuilt Doncaster from A10

To traffic   17/11/45

REPAIRS:
Don.4/4-17/5/47.**G.**
Don.25/9-8/10/47.**L.**
Don.7/8-27/9/48.**G.**
Don.15/10-23/11/50.**G.**
Don.29/10-4/12/52.**G.**
Don.24/2-11/3/54.**C/L.**
Don.15/6-29/7/54.**G.**
Don.18/1-1/3/56.**G.**
Don.19-31/1/57.**C/L.**
Don.29/1-28/2/58.**G.**
Don.28/7-8/8/59.**N/C.**
Don.16/10-3/11/59.**C/L.**
Don.13/2-30/3/60.**G.**
Don.5/2-29/3/62.**C/L.**
Don.31/7-26/9/62.**G.**
Don.30/11-21/12/62.**C/L.**

BOILERS:
 8081 (ex2599)
27013 (ex60089) 23/11/50
27028 (ex60112) 4/12/52
27080 (ex60059) 29/7/54
27056 (ex60105) 28/2/58
27033 (ex60061) 30/3/60

TENDERS:
5260 -29/10/52
5580 4/12/52-23/11/64

SHEDS:
Grantham
Kings Cross 27/10/46
Neasden 3/2/49
Grantham 15/11/53
Copley Hill 2/5/54
Heaton 15/9/57
Gateshead 5/1/58
Darlington 8/6/58
Gateshead 7/12/58
Darlington 19/6/60
Gateshead 18/12/60
Heaton 9/9/62
Darlington 2/6/63
Gateshead 15/12/63

RENUMBERED:
No.51. 24/8/46
No.60051. 25/9/48

CONDEMNED:
23/11/64.
Sold to Hughes Bolckow
North Blyth for scrap 1/65.

65 had changed from 2564 on 20th October 1946 and joined the A3 class from 23rd March 1947 but, as here, continued to wear its incorrect *KNIGHT OF THISTLE* nameplates, which were never corrected.

60044 had been rebuilt from A10 class in September 1947 and in October 1959 acquired this boiler with 'banjo' type steam collecting dome; deflectors followed in August 1961.

E50 got that BRITISH RAILWAYS style ex works on 3rd February 1948, but only carried it until 18th August 1948 when it was changed to 60050. In April at Kings Cross station it has the usual bunch of enthusiasts inspecting main line departures.

2551
PRINCE PALATINE

Rebuilt Doncaster from A1

To traffic   8/8/41

REPAIRS:
Don.2/3-22/4/43.**G.**
Don.7/8-16/9/44.**G.**
Don.5/3-5/4/46.**G.**
Don.18/9-15/10/46.**L.**
Don.10/2-7/3/47.**L.**
Don.1/5-24/6/47.**G.**
Don.26/8-7/10/48.**H/I.**
Don.11-22/3/49.**C/L.**
Don.11/4-18/5/49.**G.**
Don.8/6-21/7/50.**G.**
Don.27/2-9/4/52.**G.**
Don.5/8-3/9/53.**G.**
Don.8/3-13/4/55.**G.**
Don.22/3-3/5/57.**G.**
Don.30/6-8/7/58.**N/C.**
Don.20/10-20/11/58.**G.**
Don.30/1-11/3/60.**G.**
Don.14/8-12/10/62.**G.**
Dar.19/3-11/5/65.**C/L.**
Inv.3-26/8/65.**N/C.**

BOILERS:
 8084 (ex2595)
 9484 (New) 5/4/46
10543 (New) 21/7/50
27021 (ex60036) 9/4/52
27064 (ex60036) 3/9/53
27058 (ex60088) 13/4/55
27012 (ex60058) 20/11/58
27027 (ex60065) 11/3/60
29294 (ex60039) 12/10/62

TENDERS:
5229 8/8/41-5/8/53
5288 3/9/53-17/1/66

SHEDS:
Grantham
Copley Hill 28/9/43
New England 29/5/44
Doncaster 12/12/48
Leicester Cen. 22/5/49
Neasden 4/7/54
Leicester Cen. 5/12/54
Copley Hill 28/8/55
Heaton 15/9/57
Gateshead 5/1/58
Darlington 19/6/60
Gateshead 18/12/60
Heaton 9/9/62
Darlington 9/12/62
Heaton 2/6/63
Gateshead 16/6/63
St Margarets 25/8/63

RENUMBERED:
No.520. 5/4/46
No.52. 11/5/46
No.60052. 7/10/48

CONDEMNED:
17/1/66.
Sold to P.W.McLellan,
Langloan for scrap 20/6/66.

2552
SANSOVINO

Rebuilt Doncaster from A1

To traffic   2/9/43

REPAIRS:
Don.27/9-8/11/44.**G.**
Don.7-17/2/45.**L.**
Don.10/4-11/5/45.**L.**
Don.5/2-16/3/46.**G.**
Don.24/8-17/10/47.**G.**
Don.30/12-48-7/2/49.
Don.6-12/4/50.*Not repaired.*
Don.1/5-16/6/50.**G.**
Don.20/2-6/3/51.**N/C.**
Don.7/4-12/5/52.**G.**
Don.1/9-10/10/53.**G.**
Don.21/2-24/3/55.**G.**
Don.16/6-4/7/55.**C/L.**
Don.5/1-20/2/57.**G.**
Don.27-29/3/57.**N/C.**
Don.27/9-15/10/57.**C/L.**
Don.4/10-12/11/58.**G.**
Don.18/9-21/10/59.**C/H.**
Don.21/2-7/4/61.**G.**
Don.12-15/9/61.**C/L.**

BOILERS:
 8079 (ex2795)
 9121 (ex2500) 7/2/49
 9569 (ex106) 16/6/50
27077 (ex60039) 12/5/52
27065 (ex60080) 10/10/53
27042 (ex60092) 24/3/55
27067 (ex60041) 20/2/57
27076 (ex60096) 12/11/58
27013 (ex60050) 21/10/59
27049 (ex60041) 7/4/61

TENDERS:
5570 2/9/43-27/5/63

SHEDS:
Copley Hill
New England 26/12/44
Leicester Cen. 7/2/49
Doncaster 22/5/49
Grantham 31/5/49
Copley Hill 2/5/54
Gateshead 15/9/57
Darlington 7/12/58
Gateshead 7/6/59
Darlington 18/6/61
Gateshead 17/12/61
Heaton 9/9/62
St Margarets 21/4/63 *(On loan)*
Heaton 16/5/63

RENUMBERED:
No.521. 16/3/46
No.53. 30/11/46
No.60053. 5/2/49

CONDEMNED:
27/5/63
Cut-up Doncaster Works.

2553
PRINCE OF WALES

Rebuilt Doncaster from A1

To traffic   28/7/43

REPAIRS:
Don.1/3-5/5/45.**G.**
Don.19/9-2/11/46.**G.**
Don.9-12/11/46.**N/C.**
Don.23/2-9/4/48.**G.**
Don.28/1-20/4/50.**G.**
Don.6/10-14/11/51.**G.**
Don.15/7-14/8/52.**H/I.**
Don.10/11-17/12/53.**G.**
Don.19-23/1/54.**N/C.**
Don.7-29/10/54.**C/L.**
Don.15/7-24/8/55.**G.**
Don.7/2-8/3/57.**G.**
Don.10/7-29/8/58.**G.**
Don.9/2-18/3/60.**G.**
Don.19/10-12/11/60.**C/L.**
Don.17-27/7/61.**C/L.**
Don.22/3-10/5/62.**G.**
Don.18/4-22/5/63.**C/L.**

BOILERS:
 8253 (ex2596)
 8776 (ex86) 20/4/50
27062 (ex60084) 14/11/51
27011 (ex60092) 17/12/53
27024 (ex60060) 8/3/57
29317 (ex60099) 29/8/58
29308 (ex60022) 18/3/60
29318 (ex60085) 10/5/62

TENDERS:
5264 -28/6/64

SHEDS:
New England
Leicester Cen 6/2/49
Kings Cross 10/6/56
Grantham 16/6/57
Doncaster 8/9/63
New England 20/10/63

RENUMBERED:
No.522. 17/3/46
No.54. 23/9/46
No.60054. 9/4/48

CONDEMNED:
28/6/64.
Sold for scrap to R.A.King,
Norwich 8/64.

2554
WOOLWINDER

Rebuilt Doncaster from A1

To traffic   3/6/42

REPAIRS:
Don.8/4-6/5/43.**L.**
Don.25/1-23/2/44.**G.**
Don.15/10-24/11/45.**G.**
Don.4/6-25/7/47.**G.**
Don.24/10-14/11/47.**L.**

Don.16/5-4/6/48.**L.**
Don.3/3-21/4/49.**G.**
Don.25/12/49-17/1/50.**C/L.**
Don.28/6-4/8/50.**G.**
Don.6-10/8/50.**N/C.**
Don.4-5/4/51.**N/C.**
Don.21/10-28/11/51.**H/I.**
Don.17/8-6/10/53.**G.**
Don.30/4-11/6/55.**G.**
Don.22-28/6/55.**N/C.**
Don.11/12/56-26/1/57.**G.**
Don.5/5-17/6/58.**G.**
Don.24/9-28/10/59.**G.**
Don.12/4-6/5/60.**C/L.**
Don.31/10-25/11/60.**C/L.**

BOILERS:
 8784 (exSpare)
 9574 (New) 25/7/47
10544 (New) 4/8/50.
10544 renumbered
27063   28/11/51.
27021 (ex60052) 6/10/53
27073 (ex60084) 11/6/55
29322 (ex60109) 26/1/57
29281 (ex60101) 17/6/58
29301 (ex60033) 28/10/59

TENDERS:
5211 3/6/42-16/10/45
5283 24/11/45-3/3/49
5286 21/4/49-4/9/62

SHEDS:
Gorton
Grantham 22/11/42
Copley Hill 2/10/43
Kings Cross 16/12/44
Doncaster 4/6/50
Kings Cross 10/6/56

RENUMBERED:
No.55. 28/9/46
No.60055. 4/6/48

CONDEMNED:
4/9/61. Whilst at Doncaster
Works for repair. Cut-up
Doncaster.

2555
CENTENARY

Rebuilt Doncaster from A1

To traffic   16/8/44

REPAIRS:
Don.1-11/9/44.**N/C.**
Don.22/1-2/3/46.**G.**
Don.22/7-5/9/47.**G.**
Don.26/3-18/5/49.**G.**
Don.16/10-22/11/50.**G.**
Don.12-15/6/51.**N/C.**
Don.15/4-13/5/52.**G.**
Don.28/1-5/2/53.**N/C.**
Don.12/1-17/2/54.**G.**
Don.17-20/1/55.**N/C.**
Don.11/4-27/5/55.**C/L.**
Don.8/1-22/2/56.**G.**
Don.11/6-8/7/57.**C/L.**

Repairs:- **C/H**-Casual Heavy.   **C/L**-Casual Light.   **G**-General.   **H**-Heavy.   **H/I**-Heavy Intermediate.   **L**-Light.   **L/I**-Light Intermediate.   **N/C**-Non-Classified.
Works:- Cow - Cowlairs.   Dar - Darlington.   Don - Doncaster.   Gat - Gateshead.   Gor - Gorton.   Hay - Haymarket shed.   SRX - St Rollox.

Don.2/11-13/12/57.**G.**
Don.14-17/12/57.**N/C.**
Don.30/5-15/7/59.**G.**
Don.21/7-23/8/60.**C/L.**
Don.8/7-18/8/61.**G.**
Don.17/8-7/9/62.**C/L.**

BOILERS:
9452 (New)
9978 (New) 18/5/49
27012 (ex60052) 22/11/50
27078 (ex60106) 13/5/52
27004 (ex60093) 17/2/54
27017 (ex60091) 22/2/56
27055 (ex60074) 13/12/57
27068 (ex60076) 15/7/59

TENDERS:
5257 -6/11/57
5269 13/12/57-18/5/63

SHEDS:
Doncaster
Grantham 6/12/44
Kings Cross 27/10/46
Copley Hill 30/5/48
Doncaster 9/9/51
Grantham 7/10/51
Doncaster 25/5/52
Kings Cross 22/6/52
Grantham 15/2/53

RENUMBERED:
No.56. 10/7/46
No.60056. 18/5/49

CONDEMNED:
13/5/63. Whilst at Doncaster
Works for repair. Cut-up
Doncaster.

57
ORMONDE

Rebuilt Doncaster from A10

To traffic   11/1/47

REPAIRS:
Don.5/5-16/6/48.**G.**
Don.10/6-28/7/49.**G.**
Don.15/11-15/12/50.**G.**
Don.1/9-10/10/52.**G.**
Hay.25/1-5/2/54.**C/L.**
Don.15/3-22/4/54.**H/I.**
Don.2/8-17/9/55.**G.**
Don.22/2-2/4/57.**G.**
Don.25/9-25/10/57.**C/L.**
Don.18/3-23/4/58.**C/L.**
Don.10/7-19/9/58.**G.**
Don.9/12/59-27/1/60.**G.**
Don.13-15/12/60.**N/C.**
Don.27/7-21/9/61.**G.**
Don.8/4-9/5/63.**C/L.**
Cow.5/7-1/8/63.**N/C.**

BOILERS:
8083 (ex2746). *8083
renumbered 27019 15/12/50.*
27012 (ex60056) 10/10/52
27030 (ex60073) 2/4/57
29290 (ex60001) 27/1/60
29323 (ex60021) 21/9/61

TENDERS:
5273 -5/5/48
5284 16/6/48-15/11/50
5281 15/12/50-28/10/63

SHEDS:
Haymarket
Carlisle Canal 23/4/61
Haymarket 15/5/61
St Margarets 13/12/61

RENUMBERED:
No.60057. 16/6/48

CONDEMNED:
28/10/63.
Sold for scrap to Arnott
Young, Carmyle 6/64.

2557
BLAIR ATHOL

Rebuilt Doncaster from A10

To traffic   8/12/45

REPAIRS:
Don.3/3-20/4/47.**G.**
Don.19/10-13/11/47.**L.**
Don.26/1-10/3/49.**G.**
Don.14-17/3/49.**N/C.**
Don.15/1-14/2/51.**G.**
Don.28/1-30/3/53.**G.**
Don.10/8-21/9/54.**H/I.**
Don.10/4-3/5/56.**C/L.**
Don.11/3-17/4/57.**G.**
Don.21/8-3/10/58.**G.**
Don.9-12/8/60.**N/C.**
Don.16/11-30/12/60.**G.**

BOILERS:
8251 (ex2393)
8250 (ex45) 10/3/49
27029 (ex60095) 14/2/51
27012 (ex60057) 17/4/57
27051 (ex60046) 3/10/58
27017 (ex60105) 30/12/60

TENDERS:
5271 -19/12/53
5289 19/12/53-16/2/55
5643 16/2/55-19/6/63

SHEDS:
Doncaster
Kings Cross 1/10/50
Doncaster 29/10/50
Copley Hill 13/6/54
Gateshead 15/9/57
Darlington 16/11/58
Gateshead 7/6/59
Darlington 17/12/61
Gateshead 24/6/62
Heaton 9/9/62

RENUMBERED:
No.58. 7/12/46
No.60058. 10/3/49

CONDEMNED:
19/6/63.
Into Doncaster Works
10/7/63 for cut-up.

2558
TRACERY

Rebuilt Doncaster from A1

To traffic   25/7/42

REPAIRS:
Don.15-29/12/42.**L.**
Don.29/12/43-28/1/44.**G.**
Don.13/8-16/10/45.**G.**
Don.4/11-14/12/46.**G.**
Don.12-26/11/47.**L.**
Don.24/5-8/7/48.**G.**
Don.26/6-18/8/49.**G.**
Don.13/11-15/12/50.**G.**
Don.3/7-8/8/52.**G.**
Don.30/6-3/7/53.*Weigh.*
Don.21/5-15/7/54.**G.**
Don.13/3-20/4/56.**G.**
Don.18/12/56-19/1/57.**C/H.**
Don.13/10-22/11/57.**G.**
Don.7-17/7/58.**C/L.**
Don.12/12/58-2/1/59.**C/L.**
Don.8/6-22/7/59.**G.**
Don.8-30/4/60.**C/L.**
Don.9/11-1/12/60.**C/L.**
Don.28/7-29/9/61.**G.**
Don.3/9-10/10/62.**C/L.**

BOILERS:
9210 (New)
8249 (ex2571) 8/7/48
9986 (New) 18/8/49
27018 (ex60048) 15/12/50
27080 (ex60087) 8/8/52
27086 (ex60081) 15/7/54
27015 (ex60085) 20/4/56
27073 (ex60055) 19/1/57
27078 (ex60036) 22/11/57
27075 (ex60088) 22/7/59

TENDERS:
5281 -14/11/50
5284 15/12/50-17/12/62

SHEDS:
Gorton
Kings Cross 29/12/42
New England 16/4/44
Kings Cross 24/9/44
Leicester Cen. 18/3/51
Kings Cross 7/4/57

RENUMBERED:
No.59. 26/10/46
No.60059. 8/7/48

CONDEMNED:
17/12/62. Whilst at
Doncaster Works for repair.
Cut-up Doncaster.

2559
THE TETRARCH

Rebuilt Doncaster from A1

To traffic   16/1/42

REPAIRS:
Don.27/5-10/7/43.**G.**
Don.27/7-2/10/45.**G.**

Don.23-30/3/46.**L.**
Don.3-20/7/46.**L.**
Don.3-12/4/47.**G.**
Don.11/8-1/10/48.**G.**
Don.28/11/49-4/1/50.**G.**
Don.13/7-15/8/51.**G.**
Don.22-31/8/51.**N/C.**
Dar.23/6-18/7/52.**C/L.**
Don.29/7-4/9/53.**G.**
Don.11/1-17/2/55.**G.**
Don.19/10/55.*Weigh.*
Gat.23-29/5/56.**N/C.**
Dar.20/8-7/9/56.**N/C.**
Don.19/1-8/3/57.**G.**
Don.30/1-14/3/59.**G.**
Don.6/7-4/8/60.**G.**

BOILERS:
9207 (New)
9446 (ex2549) 12/4/47
8777 (ex2502) 1/10/48
27054 (ex60111) 15/8/51
27069 (ex60047) 4/9/53
27024 (ex60061) 17/2/55
27042 (ex60053) 8/3/57
27021 (ex60043) 14/3/59
29278 (ex60005) 4/8/60

TENDERS:
5270 16/1/42-27/5/43
5482 10/7/43-23/9/63

SHEDS:
Gateshead
Darlington 27/1/52
Gateshead 17/8/52
Darlington 8/5/55
Gateshead 13/11/55
Darlington 26/5/57
Gateshead 1/12/57
Darlington 18/12/60
Gateshead 18/6/61
Heaton 9/9/62
Gateshead 16/6/63

RENUMBERED:
No.528. 13/4/46
No.60. 22/6/46
No.60060. 1/10/48

CONDEMNED:
23/9/63.
Into Darlington Works for
cut-up 11/10/63.

2560
PRETTY POLLY

Rebuilt Doncaster from A1

To traffic   6/5/44

REPAIRS:
Don.1/7-3/8/45.**G.**
Don.15-27/10/45.**L.**
Don.10-22/12/45.**L.**
Don.29-30/12/45.**N/C.**
Don.17-23/3/46.**L.**
Don.17/3-27/4/47.**G.**
Don.11/10-20/11/48.**G.**
Don.25/9-2/11/50.**G.**
Don.20/7-26/8/52.**G.**
Don.22-30/1/53.**N/C.**

Don.23/2-26/3/54.**G.**
Don.9-14/1/55.**N/C.**
Don.22/5-29/7/55.**G.**
Don.3-11/8/55.**N/C.**
Don.7/1-1/3/57.**G.**
Don.4-9/3/57.**N/C.**
Don.2-21/12/57.**C/H.**
Don.2/9-23/10/58.**G.**
Don.31/12/58-3/1/59.**N/C.**
Don.23/10-7/11/59.**C/L.**
Don.7-23/1/60.**C/L.**
Don.12/2-24/3/60.**G.**
Don.24/8-27/9/60.**C/L.**
Don.3/1-3/2/62.**G.**
Don.7-19/5/62.**C/L.**
Don.17/9-17/10/62.**C/L.**

BOILERS:
8781 (ex2508)
8779 (ex2577) 20/11/48
27008 (ex60068) 2/11/50
27024 (ex60069) 26/8/52
27005 (ex60068) 26/3/54
27015 (ex60059) 1/3/57
27074 (ex60086) 21/12/57
27033 (ex60083) 23/10/58
27012 (ex60052) 24/3/60
27026 (ex60078) 3/2/62

TENDERS:
5290 -8/9/63

SHEDS:
New England
Leicester Cen. 6/2/49
Doncaster 4/6/50
Copley Hill 26/11/50
Kings Cross 18/2/51
Neasden 15/7/51
Grantham 22/2/53
Kings Cross 29/8/54
Grantham 17/10/54
Doncaster 8/2/59
Kings Cross 5/4/59
New England 13/9/59
Kings Cross 8/11/59
Grantham 16/6/63

RENUMBERED:
No.61. 18/11/46
No.60061. 20/11/48

CONDEMNED:
8/9/63.
Into Doncaster Works for
cut-up 16/9/63.

2561
MINORU

Rebuilt Doncaster from A1

To traffic 24/6/44

REPAIRS:
Don.23/3-5/4/45.**L.**
Don.13/1-23/2/46.**G.**
Don.1-18/1/47.**L.**
Don.22/9-5/11/47.**G.**
Don.23/2-4/3/48.**L.**
Don.16/5-6/7/49.**G.**
Don.12-19/9/50.**C/L.**

Don.9/3-13/4/51.**G.**
Don.28/8-9/10/52.**G.**
Don.5-27/1/53.**C/L.**
Don.2/4-12/5/54.**G.**
Don.11/1/55.**N/C.**
Don.2-16/3/55.**C/L.**
Don.3/8-16/9/55.**G.**
Don.28/5-12/6/56.**N/C.**
Don.20/5-11/7/57.**G.**
Don.7-15/10/57.**C/L.**
Don.13-28/8/58.**C/L.**
Don.23/12/58-4/2/59.**G.**
Don.28/10-13/11/59.**C/L.**
Don.21/3-7/4/60.**C/L.**
Don.29/8-12/10/60.**G.**
Don.5-11/7/61.**C/L.**
Don.15/1-15/2/62.**C/L.**
Don.27/7-22/9/62.**G.**
Don.17/6-25/7/63.**C/L.**

BOILERS:
9451 (New)
9979 (New) 6/7/49
27040 (ex60055) 13/4/51
27031 (ex60093) 9/10/52
27021 (ex60055) 16/9/55
27007 (ex60103) 11/7/57
27005 (ex60073) 4/2/59
27021 (ex60060) 12/10/60
29301 (ex60055) 22/9/62

TENDERS:
5643 -19/1/46
5483 23/2/46-15/3/46
5643 15/3/46-16/2/55
5289 16/2/55-27/7/62
5211 22/9/62-26/12/64

SHEDS:
New England
Gorton 7/7/44
Kings Cross 29/10/44
Haymarket 11/4/45
Kings Cross 22/5/45
Copley Hill 30/5/48
Doncaster 9/9/51
Grantham 15/2/53
Kings Cross 25/10/53
New England 10/9/61
Grantham 16/6/63
Doncaster 8/9/63
New England 20/10/63

RENUMBERED:
No.62. 18/10/46
No.E62. 4/3/48
No.60062. 6/7/49

CONDEMNED:
26/12/64.
Sold to R.A.King, Norwich
for scrap 2/65.

2562
ISINGLASS

Rebuilt Doncaster from A10

To traffic 6/4/46

REPAIRS:
Don.8/4-15/5/47.**G.**

Don.20/12/48-21/1/49.**G.**
Don.14/9-7/10/49.**C/L.**
Don.29/1-6/3/50.**C/L.**
Don.1/2-2/3/51.**G.**
Don.8/10-13/11/52.**G.**
Don.8/6-21/7/54.**G.**
Don.5/12/55-19/1/56.**G.**
Don.24/8-7/9/56.**C/L.**
Don.14/6-1/8/57.**G.**
Don.12-18/6/58.**N/C.**
Don.25/8-5/9/58.**C/L.**
Don.29/12/58-6/2/59.**G.**
Don.2/8-22/9/60.**G.**
Don.14-16/11/60.**N/C.**
Don.8/4-6/5/61.**C/L.**
Don.15/7-10/8/61.**C/L.**
Don.1-25/1/62.**C/L.**
Don.18/6-17/8/62.**G.**
Don.22-31/10/62.**C/L.**
Don.25/4-31/5/63.**C/L.**

BOILERS:
9486 (New)
27032 (ex60069) 2/3/51
27008 (ex60061) 13/11/52
27037 (ex60065) 21/7/54
29294 (ex60018) 19/1/56
29283 (ex60095) 6/2/59
29295 (ex60025) 22/9/60
29328 (ex60036) 17/8/62

TENDERS:
5231 -28/6/64

SHEDS:
Doncaster
Kings Cross 4/6/50
Grantham 9/9/51
Neasden 22/2/53
Kings Cross 13/3/55
Neasden 25/3/56
Kings Cross 24/6/56
Grantham 16/9/56
Kings Cross 30/10/60
Grantham 16/6/63
Doncaster 8/9/63
New England 20/10/63

RENUMBERED:
No.531. 6/4/46
No.63. 3/7/46
No.60063. 21/1/49

CONDEMNED:
28/6/64.
Sold to R.A.King, Norwich
for scrap 8/64.

2563
TAGALIE

Rebuilt Doncaster from A1

To traffic 13/11/42

REPAIRS:
Cow.2-5/2/43.**L.**
Don.3/3-7/4/44.**G.**
Cow.17-19/12/44.**L.**
Don.19/9-17/11/45.**G.**
Don.8/1-11/2/47.**G.**

Don.18/12/47-30/1/48.**G.**
Don.24/5-9/7/49.**G.**
Don.25/11/50-4/1/51.**G.**
Don.14-20/6/51.**C/L.**
Don.27-29/8/52.**N/C.**
Don.4/1-6/2/53.**G.**
Don.14/8-1/10/54.**G.**
Don.26/4-20/6/56.**G.**
Don.6/12/57-10/1/58.**G.**
Don.14-28/5/58.**C/L.**
Don.26/2-7/3/59.**C/L.**
Don.14-24/3/59.**N/C.**
Don.19/5-2/6/59.**C/L.**
Don.22-25/9/59.**N/C.**
Don.4/1-10/2/60.**G.**
Don.15/9-14/10/60.**C/L.**
Don.11/4-12/5/61.**C/L.**

BOILERS:
9116 (exSpare)
9122 (ex2545) 11/2/47
9981 (New) 9/7/49
27022 (ex60082) 4/1/51
27085 (ex60053) 6/2/53
27043 (ex60047) 10/1/58
29314 (ex60013) 10/2/60

TENDERS:
5584 -4/9/61
*This tender was used 29/10/45
to 5/11/45 by A4 No.4494
whilst 2563 was in works
under repair.*

SHEDS:
Haymarket
Doncaster 2/7/50
Grantham 14/6/59

RENUMBERED:
No.64. 20/10/46
No.E64. 30/1/48
No.60064. 9/7/49

CONDEMNED:
4/9/61. Whilst at Doncaster
Works for repair. Cut-up
Doncaster.

65
KNIGHT OF THISTLE

Rebuilt Doncaster from A10

To traffic 23/3/47

REPAIRS:
Don.4/6-23/7/48.**G.**
Don.13/10-18/11/49.**G.**
Don.27/2-29/3/51.**H/I.**
Don.17/11-24/12/52.**G.**
Don.19/5-2/7/54.**G.**
Don.16/8-24/9/55.**G.**
Don.30/5-11/7/56.**C/L.**
Don.27/3-16/5/57.**G.**
Don.23/9-31/10/58.**G.**
Don.19/1-19/2/60.**G.**
Don.5-26/10/60.**C/L.**
Don.17/5-10/6/61.**C/L.**
Don.11/10-25/11/61.**G.**
Don.5/6-25/7/62.**C/L.**

Repairs:- **C/H**-Casual Heavy. **C/L**-Casual Light. **G**-General. **H**-Heavy. **H/I**-Heavy Intermediate. **L**-Light. **L/I**-Light Intermediate. **N/C**-Non-Classified.
Works:- Cow - Cowlairs. Dar - Darlington. Don - Doncaster. Gat - Gateshead. Gor - Gorton. Hay - Haymarket shed. SRX - St Rollox.

Don.30/10-23/11/62.**C/L.**
Don.12/8-16/9/63.**C/L.**

BOILERS:
9211 (ex4479)
8225 (ex2748) 23/7/48.
*8225 renumbered 27037
(29/3/51).*
27041 (ex60097) 2/7/54
27027 (ex60037) 31/10/58
27062 (ex60083) 19/2/60

TENDERS:
5276 -27/3/57
5285 16/5/57-28/6/64

SHEDS:
Haymarket
Kings Cross 2/7/50
Grantham 9/9/51
New England 17/6/62
Grantham 16/6/63
Doncaster 8/9/63
New England 20/10/63

RENUMBERED:
No.60065. 23/7/48

CONDEMNED:
28/6/64.
Sold to R.A.King, Norwich
for scrap 8/64.

2565
MERRY HAMPTON

Rebuilt Doncaster from A10

To traffic   9/12/45

REPAIRS:
Don.22-28/2/46.**L.**
Don.9/11-21/12/46.**H/I.**
Don.16/11/47-2/1/48.**G.**
Cow.8-9/2/48.**L.**
Don.6-17/3/48.**L.**
Don.18/8-6/10/49.**G.**
Don.28/2-2/4/51.**H/I.**
Don.7/12/52-14/1/53.**G.**
Don.23/3-22/4/53.**C/L.**
Don.17/12/54-27/1/55.**G.**
Don.5-11/2/55.**N/C.**
Don.31/3-24/5/57.**G.**
Don.17-5/5/6/58.**C/L.**
Don.26/8-15/10/58.**G.**
Don.12-22/1/59.**N/C.**
Don.7-28/2/59.**C/L.**
Don.7-29/1/60.**C/L.**
Don.19/5-6/7/60.**G.**
Don.28/11-21/12/60.**C/L.**
Don.18/9-13/10/61.**C/L.**
Don.1/3-19/4/62.**G.**
Don.9/1-11/2/63.**C/L.**

BOILERS:
8783 (ex2394)
9216 (ex2750) 2/1/48
8784 (ex96) 6/10/49. *8784
renumbered 27038 (2/4/51).*
27044 (ex60091) 14/1/53
29279 (ex60019) 24/5/57
29322 (ex60055) 15/10/58
29279 (ex60085) 6/7/60
29314 (ex60064) 19/4/62

TENDERS:
5211 9/12/45-17/11/47
5223 2/1/48-1/3/62
5266 19/4/62-8/9/63

SHEDS:
Haymarket
Doncaster 6/8/50
Kings Cross 1/10/50
Doncaster 29/10/50
Kings Cross 10/6/56
Doncaster 5/8/56
Kings Cross 16/6/57
Doncaster 2/11/58
Kings Cross 5/4/59
New England 13/9/59
Kings Cross 1/11/59
Grantham 16/6/63

RENUMBERED:
No.66. 7/7/46
No.60066. 17/3/48

CONDEMNED:
8/9/63.
Into Doncaster Works for
cut-up 18/9/63.

2566
LADAS

Rebuilt Doncaster from A1

To traffic   4/11/39
(with Hudd A.T.C. fitted).

REPAIRS:
Don.21/1-27/2/41.**G.**
Don.4/4-16/5/42.**G.**
Cow.13-14/7/43. *Weigh.*
Don.7/9-12/10/43.**G.**
Cow.29/11-2/12/44.**L.**
Cow.22-23/12/44.**L.**
Don.11/7-23/8/45.**G.**
Don.30/7-19/8/46.**L.**
Don.10/3-19/4/47.**G.**
Don.13-24/10/47.**L.**
Don.8-6/30/7/48.**G.**
Don.10/1-16/2/50.**G.**
Don.1/9-9/10/50.**C/L.**
Don.31/1-19/2/51.**C/L.**
Don.20/8-27/9/51.**G.**
Don.16-20/6/52.**N/C.**
Don.7/7-14/8/53.**G.**
Don.1/8-1/9/54.**N/C.**
Don.28/2-31/3/55.**G.**
Don.1-3/4/55.**N/C.**
Don.29/2-12/3/56.**N/C.**
Don.9-18/6/56.**N/C.**
Don.30/1-6/3/57.**H/I.**
Don.15/8-6/9/58.**C/L.**
Don.28/11-8/12/58.**N/C.**
Don.3/3-10/4/59.**G.**
Don.5-29/7/60.**C/L.**
Don.8/3-26/4/61.**G.**
Don.20/2-19/3/62.**C/L.**
Don.5-25/7/62.**C/L.**

BOILERS:
8226 (exSpare)
9570 (New) 19/4/47
9568 (ex36) 30/7/48
9119 (ex103) 16/2/50. *9119
renumbered 27002 (9/10/50).*

27059 (ex60102) 27/9/51
27013 (ex60051) 14/8/53
27059 (ex60036) 31/3/55
27016 (ex60049) 10/4/59
29277 (ex60031) 26/4/61

TENDERS:
5479 -29/12/62

SHEDS:
Eastfield
St Margarets 2/2/40
Haymarket 26/11/40
Kings Cross 2/7/50
Grantham 9/9/51
Doncaster 18/5/52
Kings Cross 22/6/52
Doncaster 18/10/53
Grantham 14/6/59
New England 13/9/59
Kings Cross 1/11/59

RENUMBERED:
No.67. 13/10/46
No.60067. 30/7/48

CONDEMNED:
29/12/62.
Into Doncaster Works for
cut-up 2/1/63.

60068
SIR VISTO

Rebuilt Doncaster from A10

To traffic   10/12/48

REPAIRS:
Don.21/9-25/10/50.**G.**
Don.9-19/7/51.**L.**
Don.9/7-12/8/52.**G.**
Don.1/2-3/3/54.**G.**
Don.11-28/8/56.**C/L.**
Don.8/4-24/5/57.**G.**
Don.30/8-18/9/57.**C/L.**
Don.25-30/6/58. *Weigh.*
Don.5/2-9/4/59.**G.**
Don.30/1-7/3/61.**G.**
Don.6-27/4/61.**N/C.**

BOILERS:
8721 (ex74)
27005 (New) 25/10/50. *The
original number of this boiler
was 10547.*
27036 (ex60100) 3/3/54
27031 (ex60093) 9/4/59
27029 (ex60109) 7/3/61

TENDERS:
5637 -1/2/54
5224 3/3/54-27/8/62

SHEDS:
Carlisle Canal

CONDEMNED:
27/8/62. Whilst in Doncaster
Works for repair. Cut-up
Doncaster.

2568
SCEPTRE

Rebuilt Doncaster from A1

To traffic   31/5/42

REPAIRS:
Don.17/2-18/3/44.**G.**
Don.20/9-14/10/44.**L.**
Don.19/7-15/9/45.**G.**
Don.23-29/9/45.**N/C.**
Don.4/12/46-18/1/47.**G.**
Don.7/3-29/4/49.**G.**
Don.13/12/50-19/1/51.**G.**
Don.5/6-17/7/52.**G.**
Don.6-14/10/52.**C/L.**
Don.17/11-7/12/53.**C/L.**
Don.14/4-18/5/54.**G.**
Don.25/3-30/4/55.**G.**
Don.21/6-9/8/56.**G.**
Don.27/2-1/4/58.**G.**
Don.19/3-3/4/59.**C/L.**
Don.24/8-4/9/59.**N/C.**
Don.15/2-25/3/60.**G.**
Don.27/6-26/7/60.**C/L.**

BOILERS:
9209 (New)
8252 (ex2751) 18/1/47
27024 (ex60075) 19/1/51
27020 (ex60073) 17/7/52
27025 (ex60069) 18/5/54
27049 (ex60111) 30/4/55
27063 (ex60045) 1/4/58
27040 (ex60104) 25/3/60

TENDERS:
5258 31/5/42-1/10/62

SHEDS:
York
Heaton 28/3/43
Tweedmouth 14/9/58
Copley Hill 12/6/60
Holbeck 20/11/60
Copley Hill 11/6/61
Ardsley 10/9/61

RENUMBERED:
No.537. 24/3/46
No.69. 26/5/46
No.60069. 8/7/48

CONDEMNED:
1/10/62.
Into Doncaster Works
27/5/63 for cut-up.

70
GLADIATEUR

Rebuilt Doncaster from A10

To traffic   18/1/47

REPAIRS:
Don.19/7-27/8/48.**G.**
Don.1-13/10/48.**C/L.**
Don.16-1-15/2/52.**G.**
Don.6-26/3/52.**C/L.**
Don.21/5-3/7/53.**G.**
Don.4/4-18/5/55.**G.**

60065 was changed from 65 when ex works 23rd July 1948 and the size of the figures on the cab side has been reduced from the 12″ used on 60091 to 10″ to match the lettering on the tender. In both the cab figures and those on smokebox numberplate, the sixes have the LNER's curled tail modification of true *Gill Sans*, which also applied where the figure nine was used. Fifty four A3s originally had this wrong figure style before the patterns were corrected for the remainder and subsequently sixteen which needed replacement plates changed to the correct version.

Don.21/2-23/3/57.**G.**
Don.19/12/57-8/1/58.**C/L.**
Don.3-14/11/58.**C/L.**
Don.6/3-25/4/59.**G.**
Don.14-30/3/60.**C/L.**
Don.27/7-13/9/61.**G.**

BOILERS:
 9565 (New)
 9572 (ex105) 27/8/48
 27002 (ex60067) 15/2/52
 27009 (ex60100) 3/7/53
 27064 (ex60052) 18/5/55
 27020 (ex60097) 23/3/57
 27059 (ex60067) 25/4/59
 27069 (ex60096) 13/9/61

TENDERS:
 5477 -4/5/64

SHEDS:
Gateshead
Darlington 12/12/48
Gateshead 27/1/52
Darlington 30/8/53
Gateshead 28/2/54
Darlington 5/5/57
Gateshead 3/11/57
Darlington 7/6/59
Gateshead 6/12/59
Copley Hill 12/6/60
Holbeck 20/11/60
Copley Hill 11/6/61
Ardsley 10/9/61
Neville Hill 16/6/63
Gateshead 8/12/63

RENUMBERED:
No.**60070.** 27/8/48

CONDEMNED:
4/5/64.
Sold for scrap to A.Draper,
Hull 7/64.

2570
TRANQUIL

Rebuilt Doncaster from A1

To traffic   28/10/44

REPAIRS:
Don.4-17/5/46.**G.**
Don.30/12/46-11/1/47.**C/L.**
Don.19/8-9/10/47.**G.**
Don.10-18/5/48.**N/C.**
Don.24/11-24/12/48.**G.**
Don.31/5-20/7/50.**G.**
Don.4/10-1/11/51.**G.**
Don.4/3-2/4/52.**C/L.**
Don.3/3-1/4/53.**G.**
Don.12/7-20/8/54.**G.**
Don.2-9/2/55.**N/C.**
Don.17/3-1/5/56.**G.**
Don.1-15/11/56.**C/L.**
Don.13/5-4/7/58.**G.**
Don.19/1-4/2/59.**C/L.**
Don.18/8-7/10/59.**G.**
Don.26/9-4/11/61.**G.**
Don.21/11-5/1/62.**C/H.**
Don.17-29/5/63.**C/L.**

BOILERS:
 9454 (New)
 8782 (ex2507) 24/12/48
 8720 (ex37) 20/7/50
 27061 (ex60110) 1/11/51
 27028 (ex60051) 20/8/54
 27086 (ex60059) 1/5/56
 27065 (ex60079) 4/7/58
 29329 (ex60113) 7/10/59
 29290 (ex60057) 4/11/61

TENDERS:
 5291 -15/5/63
 5263 15/5/63-12/10/64

SHEDS:
York
Neville Hill 29/9/45
Gateshead 6/5/46
Darlington 27/1/52
Gateshead 16/3/52
Darlington 5/9/54
Gateshead 13/2/55
Darlington 27/5/56
Gateshead 11/11/56
Darlington 24/2/57
Gateshead 26/5/57
Darlington 6/12/59
Gateshead 19/6/60
Heaton 9/9/62
Gateshead 16/6/63

RENUMBERED:
No.**71.** 27/10/46
No.**60071.** 18/5/48

CONDEMNED:
12/10/64.
Sold for scrap to A.Draper,
Hull 12/64.

2571
SUNSTAR

Rebuilt Doncaster from A1

To traffic   12/7/41

REPAIRS:
Don.24/6-25/7/42.**L/I.**
Don.22/1-17/2/43.**G.**
Don.6-15/5/43.**L.**
Don.12/12/44-1/2/45.**G.**
Don.14/6-27/7/46.**G.**
Don.22/1-5/3/48.**G.**
Don.16/11-1/12/48.**L.**
Don.4/7-17/8/49.**G.**
Don.22-25/8/49.**N/C.**
Don.28/3-25/4/51.**G.**
Don.30/4-5/6/52.**G.**
Don.24/11-23/12/53.**G.**
Don.27/4-7/6/55.**G.**
Don.21/11/56-5/1/57.**G.**
Don.22/4-6/6/58.**G.**
Don.13-27/8/58.**C/L.**
Don.1-18/12/58.**C/L.**
Don.7-18/7/59.**N/C.**
Don.28/10-28/11/59.**C/L.**
Don.23/4-19/5/60.**C/L.**
Don.1/9-22/11/60.**G.**

Repairs:- **C/H**-Casual Heavy. **C/L**-Casual Light. **G**-General. **H**-Heavy. **H/I**-Heavy Intermediate. **L**-Light. **L/I**-Light Intermediate. **N/C**-Non-Classified.
Works:- Cow - Cowlairs. Dar - Darlington. Don - Doncaster. Gat - Gateshead. Gor - Gorton. Hay - Haymarket shed. SRX - St Rollox.

56

BOILERS:
8249 (ex2573)
8780 (ex4481) 5/3/48
27042 (ex60092) 25/4/51
27079 (ex60076) 5/6/52
27006 (ex60090) 23/12/53
27009 (ex60070) 7/6/55
27080 (ex60051) 6/6/58

TENDERS:
5476 -22/10/62

SHEDS:
Gateshead
Heaton 28/3/43
Tweedmouth 14/9/58
Copley Hill 12/6/60
Holbeck 20/11/60
Heaton 16/7/61

RENUMBERED:
No.72. 27/7/46
No.E72. 5/3/48
No.60072. 19/8/48

CONDEMNED:
22/10/62.
Into Doncaster Works for
cut-up 22/5/63.

2572
ST GATIEN

Rebuilt Doncaster from A10

To traffic   10/11/45

REPAIRS:
Don.5/3-16/4/47.**G.**
Don.21/2-31/3/49.**G.**
Don.6/4/49.**N/C.**
Don.20/11-21/12/50.**G.**
Don.14/5-17/6/52.**G.**
Don.20/10-24/11/53.**G.**
Don.18/2-4/3/55.**N/C.**
Don.1/6-10/8/55.**G.**
Don.8/2-8/3/57.**G.**
Don.10/7-15/8/58.**G.**
Don.21-24/7/59.**N/C.**
Don.5/1-12/2/60.**G.**
Don.23/5-30/7/61.**H/I.**

BOILERS:
9117 (ex2578)
9454 (ex2570) 31/3/49.
*9454 renumbered 27020
21/12/50.*
27042 (ex60072) 17/6/52
27075 (ex60096) 24/11/53
27030 (ex60106) 10/8/55
27005 (ex60061) 8/3/57
27050 (ex60087) 15/8/58
27006 (ex60087) 12/2/60

TENDERS:
5212 -1/6/55
5278 10/8/55-19/8/63

SHEDS:
York
Heaton 6/5/46
Gateshead 16/6/63

RENUMBERED:
No.73. 27/10/46
No.60073. 31/3/49

CONDEMNED:
19/8/63.
Into Darlington Works for
cut-up 31/8/63.

2573
HARVESTER

Rebuilt Darlington from A1

To traffic   17/4/28

REPAIRS:
Dar.9-10/7/28.
Tender change.
Dar.18/2-15/3/29.**L.**
Dar.12/8-31/10/29.**G.**
Gat.5-15/5/30. *Valves.*
Gat.8-17/7/30. *Valves.*
Gat.8-22/10/30. *Valves.*
Gat.21/11-8/12/30.**L.**
Don.16/2-2/3/31.**G.**
Don.4/2-16/3/32.**G.**
Don.21/1-17/2/33.**H.**
Don.23/3-12/5/33.**G.**
Don.21/2-14/4/34.**G.**
Don.28/1-6/3/35.**G.**
Don.14/1-27/2/36.**G.**
Dar.11/7/36. *Weigh.*
Dar.6/11/36. *Weigh.*
Don.14/12/36-29/1/37.**G.**
Don.6/12/37-10/1/38.**G.**
Don.27/8-26/9/38.**L.**
Don.19/4-24/5/39.**G.**
Don.4-29/6/40.**G.**
Don.10/6-14/7/42.**G.**
Don.22/2-25/3/44.**G.**
Don.6/10-17/11/45.**G.**
Don.13/6-2/8/47.**G.**
Don.13-23/8/47.**N/C.**
Don.10-22/5/48.**L.**
Don.3/11-10/12/48.**G.**
Don.12/10-17/11/50.**G.**
Don.6/10-6/11/52.**G.**
Don.4/8-15/9/54.**G.**
Don.17-31/8/55.**C/L.**
Don.22/11/55-6/1/56.**G.**
Don.1-10/1/57.**C/L.**
Don.6-11/7/57.**C/L.**
Don.29/8-18/10/57.**G.**
Don.18-27/11/58.**N/C.**
Don.5/2-20/3/59.**G.**
Don.5-12/4/60.**N/C.**
Don.8/12/60-17/1/61.**G.**

BOILERS:
8030 (New)
8252 (New) 16/3/32
8249 (ex2578) 6/3/35
8251 (ex2745)29/6/40
8082 (exSpare) 14/7/42
8721 (exSpare) 2/8/47
9120 (ex2575) 10/12/48
27010 (ex60080) 17/11/50
27040 (ex60062) 6/11/52
27061 (ex60071) 15/9/54
27055 (ex60043) 6/1/56
27077 (ex60040) 18/10/57
27041 (ex60065) 20/3/59

TENDERS:
5325 10/4/28-2/7/28
5274 2/7/28-9/7/28
5283 10/7/28-21/5/42
5268 14/7/42-8/12/60
5271 17/1/61-8/4/63

SHEDS:
Gateshead
Haymarket 18/4/28
Gateshead 5/7/28
Haymarket 12/4/37
Gateshead 21/2/38
Neville Hill 2/12/39
York 28/2/40
Heaton 28/3/43
Gateshead 3/11/45
Neville Hill 6/2/49
York 27/11/50
Neville Hill 17/12/50

RENUMBERED:
No.542. 7/4/46
No.74. 30/6/46
No.60074. 19/5/48

CONDEMNED:
8/4/63.
Into Doncaster Works for
cut-up 29/5/63.

2574
ST FRUSQUIN

Rebuilt Doncaster from A1

To traffic   26/6/42

REPAIRS:
Don.7/7/42.**N/C.**
Don.23/9-7/10/42.**L.**
Don.21/9-16/10/43.**L.**
Don.19/6-27/7/44.**G.**
Don.6/2-9/3/46.**G.**
Don.6-15/6/46.**L.**
Don.28/8-17/10/47.**G.**
Don.18-28/5/48.**N/C.**
Don.3/3-8/4/49.**G.**
Don.6/11-5/12/50.**G.**
Gat.22-31/8/51.**C/L.**
Don.9-24/10/51.**C/L.**
Don.12/5-13/6/52.**G.**
Don.10/6-16/7/53.**C/L.**
Don.22/3-28/4/54.**G.**
Gat.27/9-7/10/55.**C/L.**
Don.12/12/55-9/2/56.**G.**
Don.4/11-6/12/57.**G.**
Don.28/4-7/5/58.**N/C.**
Don.14-25/7/58.**N/C.**
Don.21-26/3/59.**N/C.**
Don.13/7-14/8/59.**G.**
Don.23/3-12/5/61.**G.**
Don.19/3-7/4/62.**C/L.**
Don.17/12/62-4/1/63.**N/C.**

BOILERS:
9208 (New)
9123 (ex2547) 17/10/47
27016 (ex60056) 5/12/50
27017 (ex60095) 13/6/52
27079 (ex60072) 28/4/54
27046 (ex60042) 9/2/56
27004 (ex60088) 6/12/57

27073 (ex60047) 14/8/59
29324 (ex60028) 12/5/61

TENDERS:
5284 -19/6/44
5269 27/7/44-4/11/57
5257 6/12/57-17/12/62
5287 4/1/63-13/1/64

SHEDS:
Gateshead
Darlington 17/8/52
Gateshead 22/2/53
Darlington 31/10/54
Gateshead 8/5/55
Darlington 18/6/61
Gateshead 17/12/61
Darlington 24/6/62
Heaton 9/12/62
Darlington 2/6/63
Gateshead 15/12/63

RENUMBERED:
No.75. 27/10/46
No.60075. 28/5/48

CONDEMNED:
13/1/64.
Into Darlington Works for
cut-up 4/2/64.

2575
GALOPIN

Rebuilt Doncaster from A1

To traffic   27/6/41

REPAIRS:
Don.27/8-7/10/42.**G.**
Don.22/2-25/3/44.**G.**
Don.12/10-1/11/44.**L.**
Don.30/4-13/7/45.**G.**
Don.17/9-3/10/45.**L.**
Don.1-15/2/46.**L.**
Don.17/12/46-25/1/47.**G.**
Don.5-9/3/47.**N/C.**
Don.2-9/10/47.**L.**
Don.28/11-17/12/47.**L.**
Don.20/7-2/9/48.**G.**
Don.9-24/6/49.**C/L.**
Dar.9-10/9/49.**C/L.**
Dar.18-25/10/49.**C/L.**
Don.5/2-11/3/52.**G.**
Don.1-20/4/53.**H/I.**
Don.4/3-7/4/54.**G.**
Don.15/9-24/10/55.**G.**
Don.8/2-27/9/57.**G.**
Don.20-29/10/58.**N/C.**
Don.12/5-30/6/59.**G.**
Don.4-8/7/59.**N/C.**
Don.21/9-9/11/60.**G.**

BOILERS:
9120 (New)
9565 (ex70) 2/9/48
27071 (ex60071) 11/3/52
27034 (ex60083) 7/4/54
27068 (ex60037) 27/9/57
27046 (ex60086) 30/6/59
27067 (ex60097) 9/11/60

TENDERS:
5227 -22/2/44
5232 25/3/44-21/9/60
5262 9/11/60-29/10/62

SHEDS:
Gateshead
Darlington 19/12/48
Gateshead 27/1/52
Darlington 16/3/52
Gateshead 14/9/52
Darlington 12/2/56
Gateshead 19/8/56
Darlington 1/12/57
Gateshead 8/6/58
Darlington 18/12/60
Gateshead 18/6/61
Heaton 9/9/62

RENUMBERED:
No.76. 15/9/46
No.60076. 2/9/48

CONDEMNED:
29/10/62.
Into Doncaster Works for
cut-up 17/4/63.

2576
THE WHITE KNIGHT

Rebuilt Doncaster from A1

To traffic   10/7/43

REPAIRS:
Don.19/2-31/3/45.**G.**
Don.26/10-23/11/46.**G.**
Don.15-22/2/47.**L.**
Don.26/4-10/5/47.**L.**
Don.14/10-17/11/48.**G.**
Gat.25/11-20/12/48.**L.**
Front end collision.
Don.1/9-5/10/49.**C/H.**
Don.17/8-28/9/50.**L.**
Gat.20-22/3/51.**C/L.**
Don.1/2-4/3/52.**G.**
Don.28/9-5/11/53.**G.**
Don.11/5-28/6/55.**G.**
Don.15/10-30/11/56.**G.**
Don.24/12/57-1/2/58.**G.**
Don.15-24/7/58.**N/C.**
Don.9/3-1/4/59.**C/H.**
Don.20/7-15/9/59.**G.**
Don.27/10-24/11/60.**C/H.**
Don.30/5-7/7/61.**L/I.**
Dar.22/1-1/2/64.**C/L.**

BOILERS:
8078 (ex4480)
8084 (ex2551) 23/11/46
9573 (ex48) 17/11/48
27000 (ex60110) 28/9/50
27070 (ex60041) 4/3/52
27007 (ex60045) 5/11/53
27006 (ex60072) 28/6/55
27072 (ex60084) 30/11/56
27085 (ex60064) 1/2/58
27048 (ex60105) 1/4/59
27046 (ex60076) 24/11/60

TENDERS:
5270 10/7/43-28/9/53
5581 5/11/53-1/2/64
5478 1/2/64-13/7/64

SHEDS:
York
Heaton 6/5/46
Holbeck 21/2/60
Copley Hill 11/6/61
Ardsley 10/9/61
St Margarets 16/6/63

RENUMBERED:
No.545. 24/3/46
No.77. 30/6/46
No.60077. 17/11/48

CONDEMNED:
13/7/64.
Sold for scrap to Arnott
Young, Carmyle. 10/64.

2577
NIGHT HAWK

Rebuilt Doncaster from A1

To traffic   15/1/44

REPAIRS:
Don.28/6-25/8/45.**G.**
Don.13-27/7/46.**L.**
Don.18/1-22/2/47.**G.**
Don.28/9-6/11/48.**G.**
Gat.24-26/8/49.**C/L.**
Gat.7-9/12/49.**N/C.**
Don.24/8-7/10/50.**G.**
Don.10-12/10/50.**N/C.**
Don.3/4-6/5/52.**G.**
Don.25/9-21/10/52.**C/L.**
Don.22/7-28/8/53.**G.**
Don.27/9-3/11/54.**G.**
Don.14/4-5/6/56.**G.**
Don.5-16/3/57.**C/L.**
Don.25/11/57-2/1/58.**G.**
Don.9-16/7/58.**N/C.**
Don.5/1-27/2/59.**G.**
Don.11/10-14/11/60.**G.**
Don.29/8-23/9/61.**C/L.**
Don.16/1-8/3/62.**C/H.**

BOILERS:
8779 (ex2503)
9446 (ex60) 6/11/48
27001 (New) 7/10/50
27014 (ex60082) 6/5/52
27001 (ex60040) 28/8/53
27028 (ex60071) 5/6/56
27017 (ex60056) 2/1/58
27070 (ex60035) 27/2/59
27007 (ex60049) 14/11/60

TENDERS:
5287 -3/4/52
5275 6/5/52-22/10/62

SHEDS:
York
Neville Hill 29/9/45
Gateshead 6/5/46

Darlington 13/2/55
Gateshead 7/8/55
Heaton 9/9/62

RENUMBERED:
No.78. 10/11/46
No.60078. 10/4/48

CONDEMNED:
22/10/62.
Into Doncaster Works for
cut-up 9/5/63.

2578
BAYARDO

Rebuilt Darlington from A1

To traffic   22/5/28

REPAIRS:
Gat.14-23/6/28.**L.**
Dar.22/2-21/5/29.**G.**
Dar.22/10-31/12/29.**H.**
Don.5/5-27/6/30.**G.**
Don.25/9-5/11/31.**G.**
Don.2-5/2/32.**L.**
Don.17/11-28/12/32.**G.**
Dar.24/2-13/4/33.**L.**
Dar.9-17/5/33.**N/C.**
Don.18/9-6/11/33.**G.**
Don.7/11-15/12/34.**G.**
Don.28/3-18/4/35.**L.**
Dar.3/12/35. *Weigh.*
Dar.16-19/12/35.**L.**
Don.28/1-14/3/36.**G.**
Don.2/3-10/4/37.**G.**
Dar.13/5/37. *Weigh.*
Dar.19-23/7/37.**N/C.**
Don.23/2-1/4/38.**G.**
Don.17/4-13/5/39.**G.**
Don.15/5-15/6/40.**G.**
Don.16-23/12/40.**L.**
Don.17/12/41-16/1/42.**G.**
Don.12/8-9/9/43.**G.**
Don.29/12/43-22/1/44.**L.**
Don.10/3-21/4/45.**G.**
Don.27/10-29/12/45.**G.**
Don.15/2-29/3/47.**G.**
Don.2/2-20/3/48.**G.**
Don.25/4-12/5/49.**L.**
Gat.7-11/11/49.**N/C.**
Don.11/4-19/5/50.**G.**
Don.4-31/1/52.**G.**
Don.17/7-12/8/52.**C/L.**
Don.23/10-4/11/52.**C/L.**
Don.28/7-6/10/53.**G.**
Don.13/12/54-20/1/55.**G.**
Don.23/1-14/2/56.**C/L.**
Don.20/9-14/11/56.**G.**
Don.8/5-12/6/58.**G.**
Don.6-18/4/59.**C/L.**
Don.25/11/59-1/1/60.**G.**

BOILERS:
8031 (New)
8249 (ex2598) 28/12/32
8226 (ex2795) 15/12/34
8027 (ex2743) 14/3/36
9117 (New) 15/6/40
8247 (ex2749) 21/4/45

9570 (ex43) 19/5/50. *9570
renumbered 27066 31/1/52.*
27050 (ex60105) 6/10/53
27065 (ex60096) 14/11/56
27000 (ex60102) 12/6/58
27026 (ex60084) 1/1/60

TENDERS:
5288 -22/2/38
5277 1/4/38-11/9/61

SHEDS:
Heaton
Doncaster 23/8/37
Haymarket 11/9/37
Heaton 31/1/38
Gateshead 22/1/40
Heaton 6/1/45
Gateshead 28/5/45
Carlisle Canal 30/5/48

RENUMBERED:
No.79. 7/11/46
No.60079. 18/3/48

CONDEMNED:
11/9/61 whilst at Doncaster
Works for repair. Cut-up
Doncaster.

2579
DICK TURPIN

Rebuilt Doncaster from A1

To traffic   26/11/42

REPAIRS:
Don.2-14/9/43.**L.**
Don.20/7-17/8/44.**G.**
Don.9-14/11/44.**N/C.**
Don.29/12/45-2/2/46.**G.**
Don.26/10-2/11/46.**L.**
Don.23/6-9/8/47.**G.**
Don.7/2-18/3/49.**G.**
Don.14/9-20/10/50.**G.**
Don.7/1-5/2/52.**G.**
Don.5/8-4/9/53.**G.**
Don.28/1-1/3/55.**G.**
Don.20/10-11/11/55.**C/L.**
Don.30/5-19/7/56.**G.**
Don.16/4-8/5/57.**C/L.**
Don.30/5-7/6/57.**C/L.**
Don.23-31/7/57.**C/L.**
Don.4/2-21/3/58.**G.**
Don.29/8-13/10/59.**G.**
Don.3-29/10/60.**C/L.**
Don.23/9-3/11/61.**G.**
Dar.25/1-14/2/64.**L.**

BOILERS:
8778 (exSpare)
9207 (ex60) 9/8/47
27003 (ex60077) 20/10/50
27065 (ex60097) 5/2/52
27002 (ex60070) 4/9/53
27069 (ex60060) 1/3/55
27082 (ex60041) 21/3/58
27065 (ex60071) 13/10/59
27079 (ex60092) 3/11/61

Repairs:- **C/H**-Casual Heavy. **C/L**-Casual Light. **G**-General. **H**-Heavy. **H/I**-Heavy Intermediate. **L**-Light. **L/I**-Light Intermediate. **N/C**-Non-Classified.
Works:- Cow - Cowlairs. Dar - Darlington. Don - Doncaster. Gat - Gateshead. Gor - Gorton. Hay - Haymarket shed. SRX - St Rollox.

TENDERS:
5288 -5/8/53
5229 4/9/53-12/10/64

SHEDS:
Heaton
Gateshead 31/8/44
Heaton 3/11/45
Holbeck 8/5/60
Ardsley 11/6/61
Neville Hill 16/6/63
Gateshead 8/12/63

RENUMBERED:
No.80. 2/11/46
No.60080. 18/3/49

CONDEMNED:
12/10/64.
Sold for scrap to A.Draper, Hull. 12/64.

2580
SHOTOVER

Rebuilt Darlington from A1

To traffic   16/2/28

REPAIRS:
Dar.13-20/4/28.**N/C.**
Dar.25/10-29/11/28.**L.**
Gat.6-8/2/29. *Valves.*
Dar.27/2/29.*Tender change.*

Dar.18/4-20/7/29.**G.**
A.C.F.I. fitted.
Dar.14-24/10/29.**N/C.**
Gat.25-29/11/29.**L.**
Dar.11/4-16/5/30.**L.**
Alteration to A.C.F.I. pump.
Don.5/2-27/3/31.**G.**
Dar.9-26/10/31.**N/C.**
Don.25/8-20/10/32.**G.**
Dar.17/2-31/3/33.**L.**
Dar.11/7-2/8/33.**N/C.**
Dar.9-16/3/34.**N/C.**
Alteration to A.C.F.I. pump.
Don.13-22/6/34.**L.**
Dar.18/9-3/10/34.**N/C.**
Don.29/10-6/12/34.**G.**
Don.6/12/35-25/1/36.**G.**
Don.17/9-28/10/36.**G.**
Don.1-30/10/37.**G.**
Don.3-13/5/38.**L.**
Don.24/8-1/9/38.**L.**
Don.21/12/38-4/2/39.**G.**
A.C.F.I. removed.
Don.5-27/4/40.**G.**
Don.3/6-4/7/41.**G.**
Don.2-7/2/42.**L.**
Don.31/8-25/9/43.**G.**
Don.14/4-2/6/45.**G.**
Dar.30/5/46. *Weigh.*
Don.24/8-12/10/46.**G.**
Don.24-31/5/47.**L.**
Don.13/4-3/6/48.**G.**
Don.25/8-14/10/49.**G.**
Dar.13/9/50. *Weigh.*
Don.30/5-6/7/51.**G.**
Don.22-25/4/52.**N/C.**

Don.12/1-12/2/53.**G.**
Don.30/4-8/6/54.**G.**
Don.19/7-16/9/55.**G.**
Don.14/7-2/8/56.**C/L.**
Don.19/12/56-1/2/57.**G.**
Don.23/8-5/9/57.**C/L.**
Don.20/8-31/10/58.**G.**
Don.17-19/3/59.**N/C.**
Don.10/9-15/10/60.**G.**

BOILERS:
8029 (New)
8079 (ex2747) 20/10/32
8080 (ex4480) 6/12/34
8076 (ex2752) 25/1/36
8224 (ex2544) 28/10/36
8721 (ex2597) 4/7/41
9514 (New) 12/10/46
27051 (ex60063) 6/7/51
27086 (ex60072) 12/2/53
27054 (ex60060) 8/6/54
29283 (ex60063) 15/10/60

TENDERS:
5290 -13/4/28
5326 20/4/28-27/2/29
5290 27/2/29-15/9/36
5286 28/10/36-13/12/38
5280 4/2/39-13/4/48
5273 3/6/48-1/10/62

SHEDS:
Heaton
Gateshead 29/9/28
Heaton 5/3/30
Neville Hill 2/12/39

York 28/2/40
Heaton 28/3/43
Gateshead 3/11/45
Neville Hill 6/2/49

RENUMBERED:
No.81. 1/12/46
No.60081. 3/6/48

CONDEMNED:
1/10/62.
Into Doncaster Works for cut-up 28/5/63.

2581
NEIL GOW

Rebuilt Doncaster from A1

To traffic   15/1/43

REPAIRS:
Don.6-13/5/43.**L.**
Don.13-26/9/43.**L.**
Don.11/11-16/12/44.**G.**
Don.10-17/4/45.**L.**
Don.18/5-22/6/46.**G.**
Don.5/4-29/5/48.**G.**
Don.8/8-24/9/49.**G.**
Gat.27/9-2/10/50.**L.**
Don.23/10-24/11/50.**G.**
Don.28/2-28/3/52.**G.**
Don.16/2-17/3/54.**G.**
Don.2/5-11/6/55.**G.**
Don.10-29/11/55.**N/C.**

60066 is of interest, for from January 1948 it was fitted with the cab with the prominent ventilator which started off in 1923 on A1 class 1481N. Its own cab had been wrecked in the derailment at Goswick in October 1947. 60066 did not have smokebox number plate fitted until October 1949, and by then true *Gill Sans* sixes were in use.

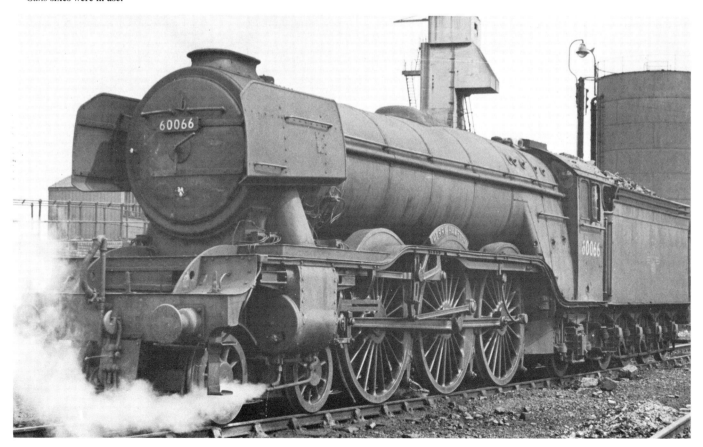

Don.5/9-2/11/56.**H/I.**
Don.14/2-21/3/58.**G.**
Don.7/8-18/9/59.**G.**
Don.19/7-25/8/61.**G.**
Don.13-22/11/62.**C/L.**

BOILERS:
9212 (New)
8078 (ex103) 29/5/48
8226 (ex60044) 24/9/49
27014 (ex60090) 24/11/50
27074 (ex60091) 28/3/52
27000 (ex60106) 17/3/54
27062 (ex60090) 11/6/55
27015 (ex60061) 21/3/58
27078 (ex60059) 18/9/59
29310 (ex60022) 25/8/61

TENDERS:
5272 15/1/43-11/11/44
5226 16/12/44-2/9/63

SHEDS:
Heaton
Gateshead 13/6/48
Darlington 14/9/52
Gateshead 22/3/53
Heaton 6/5/56
Holbeck 8/5/60
Heaton 16/7/61
Gateshead 25/3/62
Heaton 9/9/62
Gateshead 16/6/63

RENUMBERED:
No.82. 20/6/46
No.60082. 26/5/48

CONDEMNED:
2/9/63.
Into Darlington Works for
cut-up 22/2/64.

2582
SIR HUGO

Rebuilt Doncaster from A1

To traffic   17/12/41

REPAIRS:
Don.6/9-1/10/43.**G.**
Don.7/2-17/3/45.**G.**
Don.15/6-17/8/46.**G.**
Don.15/9-25/10/47.**G.**
Don.20/4-28/5/49.**G.**
Don.2/2-15/3/51.**G.**
Don.29/7-2/9/52.**G.**
Don.10/2-12/3/54.**G.**
Don.26/5-8/7/55.**G.**
Don.8/11-12/12/56.**G.**
Don.28/3-10/4/57.**C/L.**
Don.7/5-17/6/58.**G.**
Don.18/8-2/9/59.**C/L.**
Don.5/1-12/2/60.**G.**
Don.21/4-11/5/61.**N/C.**
Don.5/1-8/2/62.**G.**

BOILERS:
8027 (ex2578)
9513 (New) 17/8/46

27034 (ex60078) 15/3/51
27016 (ex60084) 12/3/54
27035 (ex60040) 8/7/55
27033 (ex60044) 12/12/56
27062 (ex60082) 17/6/58
27030 (ex60057) 12/2/60
29309 (ex60087) 8/2/62

TENDERS:
5282 -11/5/64

SHEDS:
Heaton
Gatehead 16/6/63

RENUMBERED:
No.83. 20/10/46
No.60083. 27/5/49

CONDEMNED:
18/5/64.
Sold for scrap to Hughes
Bolckow, North Blyth 8/64.

4471
*SIR FREDERICK
BANBURY*

Rebuilt Doncaster from A1

To traffic   16/10/42

REPAIRS:
Don.15/7-5/9/43.**G.**
Don.18/6-25/8/45.**G.**
Don.11/4-20/5/47.**G.**
Don.26/9-8/10/47.**L.**
Don.28/3-13/5/49.**G.**
Don.5/7-10/8/51.**G.**
Don.25/2-28/3/53.**H/I.**
Don.14/8-30/9/53.**C/L.**
Don.27/4-16/6/55.**G.**
Don.13/6/56. *Weigh.*
Don.1/11-14/12/56.**H/I.**
Don.11/4-6/6/58.**G.**
Don.13-21/4/59.**N/C.**
Don.7/5-3/6/59.**C/L.**
Don.28/9-8/10/59.**N/C.**
Don.5/4-19/5/60.**G.**
Don.14/11-3/12/60.**C/L.**
Don.6-24/3/61.**C/L.**
Don.19/7-9/8/61.**C/L.**

BOILERS:
8248 (ex2544)
9571 (New) 20/5/47
27052 (ex60083) 10/8/51
27000 (ex60082) 16/6/55
27001 (ex60089) 6/6/58
29285 (ex60032) 19/5/60

TENDERS:
5292 16/10/42-14/11/61

SHEDS:
Doncaster
Grantham 1/7/43
New England 30/4/44
Grantham 11/10/44
Leicester Cen. 16/5/49
Neasden 4/7/54

Leicester Cen. 21/11/54
Kings Cross 1/9/57
Doncaster 13/10/57
Grantham 14/6/59
Kings Cross 9/10/60

RENUMBERED:
No.102. 24/8/46
No.60102. 13/5/49

CONDEMNED:
14/11/61.
Into Doncaster Works for
cut-up 14/11/61.

103
FLYING SCOTSMAN

Rebuilt Doncaster from A10

To traffic   4/1/47

REPAIRS:
Don.2/2-15/3/48.**G.**
Don.17-30/12/48.**L.**
Don.4/11-16/12/49.**G.**
Don.5/2-14/3/52.**G.**
Don.8/3-6/4/54.**G.**
Don.13-22/4/54.**N/C.**
Don.26/8-8/10/55.**G.**
Don.6/5-13/7/57.**G.**
Don.10/12/58-24/1/59.**G.**
Don.8-24/3/60.**C/L.**
Don.6/7-9/8/60.**G.**
Don.14/2-4/3/61.**C/L.**
Don.21/11-16/12/61.**C/L.**
Don.25/4-2/6/62.**G.**

BOILERS:
8078 (ex2576)
9119 (ex2505) 15/3/48
9448 (ex2747) 16/12/49
27015 (ex60047) 14/3/52
27074 (ex60082) 6/4/54
27007 (ex60077) 8/10/55
27011 (ex60054) 13/7/57
27044 (ex60097) 24/1/59
27047 (ex60100) 9/8/60
27058 (ex60037) 2/6/62

TENDERS:
5640 -15/1/63
5325 *For preservation.*

SHEDS:
Doncaster
Leicester Cen. 4/6/50
Grantham 15/11/53
Kings Cross 20/6/54
Grantham 29/8/54
Kings Cross 7/4/57

RENUMBERED:
No.E103. 15/3/48
No.60103. 30/12/48

WITHDRAWN:
15/1/63.
Sold for preservation
to A.F.Pegler.

4473
SOLARIO

Rebuilt Doncaster from A1

To traffic   11/10/41

REPAIRS:
Don.2/1-5/2/43.**G.**
Don.21-28/8/43.**L.**
Don.15/4-24/5/44.**G.**
Don.4/12/45-26/1/46.**G.**
Don.2/12/46-25/1/47.**G.**
Don.5/6-28/7/48.**G.**
Don.6/12/49-13/1/50.**G.**
Don.10/1-21/2/51.**G.**
Don.11/5-17/6/53.**G.**
Don.2-29/9/53.**C/L.**
Don.11/5-1/7/55.**G.**
Don.4-6/7/55.**N/C.**
Don.17/1-17/2/56.**C/L.**
Don.16/11-29/12/56.**G.**
Don.3-5/1/57.**N/C.**
Don.6/3-18/4/58.**G.**
Don.19-23/4/58.**N/C.**
Don.24/2/59. *Weigh.*
Don.12-17/3/59.**N/C.**
Don.13-24/4/59.**C/L.**
Don.16/6-4/7/59.**N/C.**

BOILERS:
9123 (New)
9483 (New) 26/1/46
27030 (ex60041) 21/2/51
27010 (ex60074) 17/6/53
27052 (ex60102) 1/7/55
27035 (ex60083) 29/12/56
27040 (ex60038) 18/4/58

TENDERS:
5254 -7/12/59

SHEDS:
Gorton
Kings Cross 5/2/43
Leicester Cen. 4/6/50
Neasden 4/7/54
Leicester Cen. 26/12/54
Kings Cross 1/9/57
Doncaster 13/10/57
Grantham 14/6/59
Kings Cross 1/11/59

RENUMBERED:
No.104. 12/5/46
No.60104. 28/7/48

CONDEMNED:
7/12/59.
Entered Doncaster Works
for repair 19/11/59. Cut-up
12/59.

4474
VICTOR WILD

Rebuilt Doncaster from A1

To traffic   1/10/42

Repairs:- **C/H**-Casual Heavy.   **C/L**-Casual Light.   **G**-General.   **H**-Heavy.   **H/I**-Heavy Intermediate.   **L**-Light.   **L/I**-Light Intermediate.   **N/C**-Non-Classified.
Works:-   Cow - Cowlairs.   Dar - Darlington.   Don - Doncaster.   Gat - Gateshead.   Gor - Gorton.   Hay - Haymarket shed.   SRX - St Rollox.

REPAIRS:
Don.13-30/3/43.**L.**
Don.19/10-20/11/43.**L.**
Don.6/5-3/6/44.**G.**
Don.7/9-7/10/44.**L.**
Don.1/11-7/12/45.**G.**
Don.18/4-31/5/47.**G.**
Don.2/7-18/8/48.**G.**
Don.15/1-17/3/50.**G.**
Don.16/8-1/9/50.**C/L.**
Don.21/11-7/12/50.**C/L**
Don.21/5-3/7/51.**G.**
Don.11-17/7/51.**N/C.**
Don.18/1-20/2/53.**G.**
Don.6/7-13/8/54.**G.**
Don.12/10-9/12/55.**H/I.**
Don.19/7-17/8/56.**C/L.**
Don.11/6-10/8/57.**G.**
Don.27/1-6/3/59.**G.**
Don.22/2-5/3/60.**C/L.**
Don.1/11-9/12/60.**G.**
Don.30/8-29/9/61.**C/L.**
Don.17/9-18/10/62.**C/L.**
Don.6/2-8/3/63.**N/C.**

BOILERS:
8076 (ex2796)
9572 (New) 31/5/47
9212 (ex2581) 18/8/48
9216 (ex66) 17/3/50
27050 (ex60050) 3/7/51
27051 (ex60081) 20/2/53
27056 (ex60110) 13/8/54
27048 (ex60035) 10/8/57
27017 (ex60078) 6/3/59
27070 (ex60078) 9/12/60

TENDERS:
5225 -16/6/63

SHEDS:
Gorton
Kings Cross 22/11/42
Grantham 9/9/51

RENUMBERED:
No.105. 12/5/46
No.60105. 18/8/48

CONDEMNED:
16/6/63.
Into Doncaster Works for
cut-up 22/8/63.

106
FLYING FOX

Rebuilt Doncaster from A10

To traffic   15/3/47

REPAIRS:
Don.18/10-3/12/48.**G.**
Don.8/4-24/5/50.**G.**
Don.14/6-6/7/51.**C/L.**
Don.13/3-20/4/52.**G.**
Don.3/11-10/12/53.**G.**
Don.16/6-26/7/55.**G.**
Don.3-6/10/55.**N/C.**
Don.5/6-6/7/56.**C/L.**
Don.19/1-22/2/57.**H/I.**
Don.11-26/3/58.**C/H.**

Don.29/9-21/11/58.**G.**
Don.8/3-12/4/60.**G.**
Don.7/11-1/12/60.**C/L.**
Don.12/9-7/10/61.**C/L.**
Don.3/5-16/6/62.**G.**
Don.10/6-18/7/63.**C/L.**

BOILERS:
9569 (New)
9208 (ex39) 24/5/50
27000 (ex60077) 20/4/52
27030 (ex60104) 10/12/53
27002 (ex60080) 26/7/55
27063 (ex60069) 12/4/60
27047 (ex60103) 16/6/62

TENDERS:
5278 -16/6/55
5212 26/7/55-26/12/64

SHEDS:
New England
Grantham 9/11/47
Kings Cross 15/2/53
Grantham 25/10/53
Copley Hill 2/5/54
Leicester Cen. 28/8/55
Grantham 15/9/57
Doncaster 8/9/63
New England 20/10/63

RENUMBERED:
No.60106. 3/12/48

CONDEMNED:
26/12/64.

Sold for scrap to R.A.King,
Norwich 2/65.

4476
ROYAL LANCER

Rebuilt Doncaster from A10

To traffic   4/10/46

REPAIRS:
Don.8/3-23/4/48.**G.**
Don.20/2-30/3/49.**C/L.**
Don.20/8-10/10/49.**G.**
Don.14-19/10/49.**N/C.**
Don.25/1-1/3/50.**C/L.**
Don.2-27/4/51.**H/I.**
Don.9/10-3/12/52.**G.**
Don.11/9-20/10/54.**G.**
Don.21-23/10/54.**N/C.**
Don.7-16/8/55.**N/C.**
Don.29/2/56. *Weigh.*
Don.17/7-24/8/56.**G.**
Don.4-27/2/57.**C/L.**
Don.25/7-16/8/57.**C/L.**
Don.26/8-6/9/57.**C/L.**
Don.19/12/57-8/1/58.**C/L.**
Don.10/4-21/5/58.**G.**
Don.7/5-2/6/59.**C/L.**
Don.28/9-14/11/59.**G.**
Don.24/5-18/6/60.**C/L.**
Don.30/6-5/8/60.**C/H.**
Don.7-24/1/61.**C/L.**
Don.17/1-22/2/62.**G.**
Don.4/12/62-2/1/63.**C/L.**

68 at Edinburgh (Waverley) on 24th April 1948. It was the only one still carrying 180 lb. boiler at the demise of the LNER but from 20th March 1947 green livery and *L N E R* had been restored. Its Carlisle (Canal) shed altered the number to 60068 on Sunday 19th September 1948 but did not change the tender lettering to BRITISH RAILWAYS. On 3rd November 1948 it went into Doncaster Works and that was the end for the A1/A10 class.

E72 was changed to 60072 at Heaton shed on 19th August and out from a light repair at Doncaster on 1st December 1948 had been fitted with smokebox number plate. This had a six with curled tail and was still being carried when seen here on 1st September 1957 passing St Margarets shed on an Edinburgh - Newcastle express.

60073 *ST GATIEN*, originally an A1 class, thus had right hand drive as all 52 were so equipped, and (apart from 4470) they remained so until 1952, despite a desire to convert them twenty years earlier. The reversing rod below the running plate, and the vacuum ejector exhaust pipe along the side of the boiler gave a clear indication of which was the driving side.

60073, coming off the King Edward bridge over the Tyne on an up express, changed to left hand drive in October 1953 and the process was completed in July 1954.

BOILERS:
9515 (New) *9515 renumbered 27043 27/4/51.*
27083 (ex60048) 3/12/52
27047 (ex60048) 24/8/56
27039 (ex60044) 21/5/58
27035 (ex60044) 14/11/59
27044 (ex60097) 22/2/62

TENDERS:
5267 -1/9/63

SHEDS:
Kings Cross
Leicester Cen. 4/6/50
Copley Hill 27/7/52
Leicester Cen. 10/8/52
Grantham 15/9/57
Kings Cross 9/10/60
Grantham 16/6/63

RENUMBERED:
No.107. 4/10/46
No.60107. 23/4/48

CONDEMNED:
1/9/63.
Into Doncaster Works for cut-up 4/10/63.

4477
GAY CRUSADER

Rebuilt Doncaster from A1

To traffic   30/1/43

REPAIRS:
Don.20/12/43-1/1/44.**L.**
Don.13/10-18/11/44.**G.**
Don.21/2-28/3/46.**G.**

Don.5/7-22/8/47.**G.**
Don.7/2-25/3/49.**G.**
Don.30/7-1/9/50.**G.**
Don.17/1-21/2/52.**H/I.**
Don.29/1-5/3/53.**C/L.**
Don.23/9-30/10/53.**G.**
Don.11/10-1/11/54.**C/L.**
Don.16/5-4/7/55.**G.**
Don.6-8/7/55.**N/C.**
Don.30/5-18/7/57.**G.**
Don.3/7-15/7/58.**C/L.**
Don.4/4-21/5/59.**G.**
Don.7-24/3/60.**C/L.**
Don.13/8-21/9/60.**G.**
Don.21/3-22/4/61.**C/L.**
Don.24/10-17/11/61.**C/L.**
Don.15/2-6/4/62.**G.**
Don.4/2-1/3/63.**C/L.**

BOILERS:
9213 (New)
9124 (ex2501) 22/8/47
9210 (ex98) 1/9/50. *9210 renumbered 27068 21/2/52.*
27077 (ex60053) 30/10/53
27010 (ex60104) 4/7/55
27064 (ex60070) 18/7/57
27077 (ex60074) 21/5/59
27083 (ex60101) 21/9/60
27018 (ex60040) 6/4/62

TENDERS:
5266 -15/2/62
5223 6/4/62-19/10/63

SHEDS:
Kings Cross
Doncaster 7/1/51
Kings Cross 22/6/52
Neasden 28/9/52
Kings Cross 29/3/53
Neasden 29/11/53
Kings Cross 10/7/55

Neasden 2/10/55
Kings Cross 27/1/57
Doncaster 19/10/58
Kings Cross 2/11/58
New England 10/9/61
Grantham 16/6/63
Doncaster 8/9/63

RENUMBERED:
No.507. 28/3/46
No.108. 5/5/46
No.60108. 25/3/49

CONDEMNED:
19/10/63.
Into Darlington Works for cut-up 16/11/63.

4478
HERMIT

Rebuilt Doncaster from A1

To traffic   16/11/43

REPAIRS:
Don.22/5-13/7/45.**G.**
Don.9/1-15/3/47.**G.**
Don.9-14/5/47.**N/C.**
Don.5/3-2/5/48.**G.**
Don.30/12/48-11/1/49.**C/L.**
Don.2/10-8/11/49.**G.**
Don.6/3-5/4/51.**H/I.**
Don.23/3-24/4/52.**C/L.**
Don.16/10-27/11/52.**H/I.**
Don.27/12/53-8/1/54.**C/L.**
Don.16/10-26/11/54.**G.**
Don.3/12/56-10/1/57.**G.**
Don.14-16/1/57.**N/C.**
Don.25/2-14/3/58.**C/L.**
Don.19/1-12/3/59.**G.**

Don.2/3-5/4/60.**C/L.**
Don.10/12/60-27/1/61.**G.**
Don.15/11-12/12/61.**C/L.**
Don.22/5-8/6/62.**C/L.**
Don.4/9-29/10/62.**C/L.**

BOILERS:
9445 (new)
9116 (ex2563) 15/3/47
8080 (ex2745) 2/5/48
9451 (ex2561) 8/11/49. *9451 renumbered 27039 5/4/51.*
29322 (ex60006) 26/11/54
27052 (ex60104) 10/1/57
27029 (ex60101) 12/3/59
27973 (New) 27/1/61

TENDERS:
5289 -19/12/53
5271 19/12/53-10/12/60
5268 27/1/61-29/12/62

SHEDS:
Doncaster
Copley Hill 3/12/43
New England 29/5/44
Kings Cross 24/9/44
Grantham 9/9/51
Doncaster 18/10/53
Kings Cross 8/6/58
Doncaster 19/10/58
Kings Cross 5/4/59

RENUMBERED:
No.508. 20/1/46
No.109. 22/6/46
No.60109. 1/5/48

CONDEMNED:
29/12/62.
Into Doncaster Works for cut-up 5/4/63.

4479
ROBERT THE DEVIL

Rebuilt Doncaster from A1

To traffic   8/8/42

REPAIRS:
Don.23/2-23/3/44.**G.**
Don.30/3-4/4/44.**N/C.**
Don.8/8-6/10/45.**G.**
Don.28/12/46-8/2/47.**G.**
Don.14/1-2/3/49.**G.**
Don.19/6-3/8/50.**G.**
Don.13/7-28/8/51.**G.**
Don.20/11/52-2/1/53.**G.**
Don.13-17/2/53.**N/C.**
Don.1-10/7/53.**C/L.**
Don.25/5-13/7/54.**G.**
Don.24-27/1/55.**N/C.**
Don.28/11/55-10/1/56.**G.**
Don.25/4-8/6/57.**G.**
Don.13-14/6/57.**N/C.**
Don.4/4-30/5/59.**G.**
Don.15/8-3/9/60.**C/L.**
Don.31/1-8/3/61.**G.**
Don.11/8-13/9/61.**C/L.**
Don.10-28/4/62.**C/L.**
Don.1-31/1/63.**C/L.**

BOILERS:
9211 (New)
9566 (New) 8/2/47
9215 (ex2596) 3/8/50
27056 (ex60104) 28/8/51
27070 (ex60077) 13/7/54
27025 (ex60090) 8/6/57
27020 (ex60070) 30/5/59
27052 (ex60086) 8/3/61

TENDERS:
5230 -23/5/63. *The only A1*
to keep the same tender for
the whole of its life.

SHEDS:
New England
Grantham 11/10/42
Kings Cross 27/10/46
Grantham 9/9/51
Kings Cross 16/6/57

RENUMBERED:
No.110. 24/8/46
No.60110. 2/3/49

CONDEMNED:
23/5/63.
Into Doncaster Works for
cut-up 11/6/63.

4480
ENTERPRISE

Rebuilt Doncaster from A1

To traffic   15/7/27

REPAIRS:
Don.1-20/12/27.**L.**
Don.8-11/2/28.**L.**
Don.30/5-5/7/28.**H.**
Don.26/9-25/10/28.**H.**
Cow.8-27/3/29.**L.**
Don.5-25/7/29.**H.**
Don.19/5-14/7/30.**G.**
Don.13/10-19/12/31.**G.**
Don.7-9/6/32.**L.**
Don.2/2-5/4/33.**G.**
Don.16/5-20/6/33.**L.**
Don.11/6-10/8/34.**G.**
Don.17/8/34.**L.**
Don.22/11/35-1/2/36.**G.**
Don.9-12/2/36.**N/C.**
Don.23-25/3/36.**L.**
Don.14/2-10/4/37.**G.**
Don.28-29/10/37.**L.**
Don.22/3-9/5/38.**G.**
Don.6/5-19/6/39.**G.**
Don.31/8-23/9/39.**L.**
Don.29/3-19/4/40.**L.**
Don.7/3-25/4/41.**G.**
Don.26/11/42-11/2/43.**G.**
Don.13/11/44-3/1/45.**G.**
Don.17/3-4/5/46.**G.**
Don.14-26/11/47.**G.**
Don.8/9-28/10/49.**G.**
Don.1-3/11/49.**N/C.**
Don.11/5-20/6/51.**G.**
Don.16/1-4/3/53.**G.**
Don.4/11-5/12/53.**C/L.**

Don.27/10-9/12/54.**G.**
Don.13/2-19/4/56.**G.**
Don.9/7-15/8/57.**H/I.**
Don.11/7-2/8/58.**C/L.**
Don.1/5-5/6/59.**G.**
Don.29/6-23/9/60.**G.**
Don.1-20/5/61.**C/L.**
Don.22/3-14/4/62.**C/L.**

BOILERS:
8027 (New)
8251 (New) 14/7/30
8080 (ex2748) 5/4/33
8248 (ex2797) 10/8/34
8082 (ex2797) 1/2/36
8078 (exSpare) 25/4/41
9214 (New) 11/2/43
9452 (ex2555) 28/10/49
27049 (ex60046) 20/6/51
27023 (ex60095) 9/12/54
27025 (ex60110) 5/6/59

TENDERS:
5231 -17/2/37
5223 10/4/37-22/3/38
5477 7/5/38-6/1/45
5569 6/1/45-29/12/62

SHEDS:
Grantham
Doncaster 16/7/27
Carlisle 18/12/28
Kings Cross 5/4/29
Doncaster 14/4/29
Kings Cross 5/3/39
Grantham 31/12/41
Copley Hill 1/10/43
Grantham 11/10/43
New England 29/5/44
Doncaster 12/12/48
Neasden 20/2/49
Leicester Cen. 27/3/55
Grantham 15/9/57

RENUMBERED:
No.111. 4/5/46
No.60111. 28/10/49

CONDEMNED:
29/12/62.

Into Doncaster Works for
cut-up 3/4/63.

112
ST SIMON

Rebuilt Doncaster from A10

To traffic   30/8/46

REPAIRS:
Don.8/12/47-20/1/48.**G.**
Don.5/2-25/3/49.**G.**
Don.30/3-4/4/49.**N/C.**
Don.11/1-10/2/51.**G.**
Don.19/9-24/10/52.**G.**
Don.30-31/12/53.**N/C.**
Don.11/6-27/7/54.**H/I.**
Don.13-21/9/54.**N/C.**
Don.5/6-28/7/56.**G.**
Don.15-25/8/56.**N/C.**
Don.15/5-2/7/58.**G.**
Don.29/1-3/2/59.**N/C.**
Don.4-7/5/59.**N/C.**
Don.30/10-21/11/59.**C/L.**
Don.13/1-25/2/60.**G.**
Don.2/9-8/10/60.**C/L.**
Don.23/8-22/9/61.**C/L.**
Don.24/1-6/2/62.**C/L.**
Don.18/7-5/10/62.**G.**

BOILERS:
8780 (ex2506)
8783 (ex2565) 20/1/48
9453 (ex2744) 25/3/49
27028 (ex60096) 10/2/51
27045 (ex60050) 24/10/52
27026 (ex60093) 28/7/56
27086 (ex60071) 2/7/58
27009 (ex60096) 25/2/60
29295 (ex60063) 5/10/62

TENDERS:
5223 -10/12/47
5211 20/1/48-18/7/62
5289 5/10/62-26/12/64

SHEDS:
Kings Cross
Copley Hill 4/6/50
Doncaster 26/11/50
Copley Hill 1/4/51
Doncaster 9/9/51
Grantham 7/10/51
Doncaster 15/2/53
Grantham 14/6/59
Doncaster 8/9/63
New England 30/10/63

RENUMBERED:
No.E112. 20/1/48
No.60112. 25/3/49

CONDEMNED:
26/12/64.
Sold for scrap to R.A.King,
Norwich 2/65.

Repairs:- **C/H**-Casual Heavy.   **C/L**-Casual Light.   **G**-General.   **H**-Heavy.   **H/I**-Heavy Intermediate.   **L**-Light.   **L/I**-Light Intermediate.   **N/C**-Non-Classified.
Works:- Cow - Cowlairs.   Dar - Darlington.   Don - Doncaster.   Gat - Gateshead.   Gor - Gorton.   Hay - Haymarket shed.   SRX - St Rollox.

64

60110 - ex works to that number on 2nd March 1949 - shows that the Paint Shop had got the word about correcting the figure 6 but the smokebox plate must have been cast ere it had reached the Pattern Shop and the Foundry.

E112 arriving in Kings Cross with *The Yorkshire Pullman* is as out-shopped 20th January 1948 from a general repair, during which its cab was changed to one having ventilator of normal height above the cab roof. The cab with taller ventilator which it had carried from new, had been transferred to No.66.

4476 was equal first with 4472 to have corridor tender attached from 5th April 1928. This view clearly shows that the original batch of ten built in 1928 did have a single coal rail, a detail only rarely appreciated.

Tender 5325, the third of the corridor types. It was paired with 2573 for just eleven weeks in 1928.

PART FOUR

TENDERS

DONCASTER TENDER NUMBERS OF THOSE COUPLED TO PACIFIC TYPE ENGINES

G.N.R. DESIGN OF 1922

(WITH TWO COAL RAILS ALL ROUND)

5211	5212	5223	5224	5225	5226	5227	5228	5229	5230
5231	5232	5253	5254	5255	5256	5257	5258	5259	5260
5261	5262	5263	5264	5265	5266	5267	5268	5269	5270
5271	5272	5273	5274	5275	5276	5277	5278	5279	5280
5281	5282	5283	5284	5285	5286	5287	5288	5289	5290
5291	5292								

Total 52.

1928 CORRIDOR TYPE

(FOR NON-STOP LONDON TO EDINBURGH WORKING)

| 5323 | 5324 | 5325 | 5326 | 5327 | 5328 | 5329 | 5330 | 5331 | 5332 |

Total 10.

1930 HIGH SIDED NON-CORRIDOR TYPE

5476	5477	5478	5479	5480	5481	5482	5483	5566	5567
5568	5569	5570	5571	5572	5573	5574	5580	5581	5582
5583	5584								

Total 22

1936 NON-CORRIDOR TYPE

(WITH STREAMLINED FRONT END)

| 5636 | 5637 | 5638 | 5639 | 5640 | 5641 | 5642 | 5643 | 5644 | 5645 |

Total 10.

'Back to the cushions' following a stint at the regulator (that is, some 200 miles)

67

Great Northern coal rail tender of 1922, at New England, April 1959.

60085 at Heaton shed on 22nd March 1963. It had its final general repair and painting ex works 27th April 1962 and within less than a year its tender had lost all evidence of identity, whilst local cleaning had been needed to reveal the cab side number. This rear view is useful in showing the addition of three footsteps and a short handrail on the G.N. design tender, a facility they lacked until shopped from September 1953. Note also that this tender still retained the twin lamp irons which were redundant even before the LNER came into existence. Warning flashes have been applied to emphasize the danger of live overhead electric wiring to anyone climbing on to the tender.

2580 having changed to A3 class and to corridor tender, is going through the 'goalposts' at Craigentinny carriage sidings, south of Edinburgh, which checked for loading gauge acceptance by the non-stop engines. That erection long survived the non-stop running.

2745 new on 8th September 1928, worked from Doncaster shed but only until 26th October, when it transferred to Carlisle for the principal trains on the Waverley Route, where a heavy corridor tender was an unwanted encumbrance. It still had that type tender here at Carlisle on 27th March 1929 when detached from a train it had brought in from Edinburgh, and was on its way to Canal shed. On 30th June 1930, whilst at Haymarket shed, it exchanged tenders with almost new 2796 and the latter then became a regular non-stop worker until deposed by A4 No.4486, which took over its corridor tender in turn.

Tender 5636, the first of the non-corridor types with streamlined front end. Newcastle Central.

Pacific tenders, Kings Cross 10th March 1963.

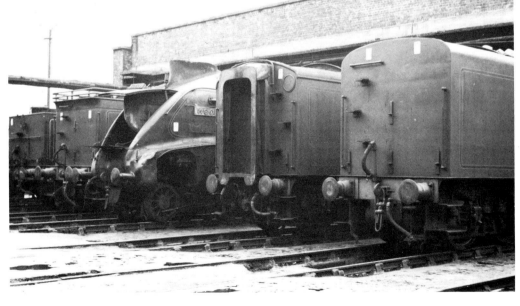

69

Brand new 5329 outside Doncaster Paint Shop 1928

2503 never ran in traffic as depicted here. In July 1935, whilst at Doncaster for a general repair, its tender front was built up and flexibly attached to the cab roof. This was an experiment brought to fruition when the A4 class first appeared some two months later.

2505 in Doncaster, May 1935 for a light repair, was used temporarily for a mock-up of a provisional cab design for the streamlining of the A4 class. As engineers well know, *if it doesn't look right, then it isn't right!* **2503's** photograph shows real improvement.

60042 an early recipient of cast numberplate on the smokebox door in its first B.R. painting, ex Doncaster works, on 12th August 1948. This view clearly shows the change to the rectangular sliding plate covering the access to the centre valve gear, also that the less useful long guard irons had not yet been removed.

2564's name, as this shows proof, was originally *KNIGHT OF THE THISTLE*, and when replacement plates were cast in December 1932, a mistake was made in dropping the definite article. It has always been an un-resolved question whether the name was that of a racehorse, because no Classic winner was so-called, although one with that name did win the 1897 Royal Hunt Cup.

PART FIVE

SOME MORE DETAIL

2743 ex works 16th March 1938 had been fitted with this Stone-Deuta speed recorder. It was driven off the trailing coupling pin, but no others were so equipped, and removal date from 2743 has not been discovered.

2567 during a three-day visit to Cowlairs in June 1930, was fitted with tablet exchange apparatus, for use without stopping on the short stretch of single line at Usan, south of Montrose. This enabled it to work to Aberdeen where it is being turned at Ferryhill shed.

2567's cab view, taken in July 1939, was in connection with its fitting with 'Hudd' Automatic Train Control, for use on the Edinburgh to Glasgow (Queen Street) line. Sadly, development of this promising safety feature was stifled by the outbreak of the War.

2506 during its June/July 1939 general repair was equipped with 'Hudd' Automatic Train Control apparatus, the receiver for which is seen between the bogie dust shields. Due to the 1939-45 war, this promising system could not then be developed, but ultimately it did form the basis on which the British Railways A.W.S. reached success.

60112 *ST SIMON* here at Grantham shed on 21st April 1960 was one of the four - the others were 60048, 60055 and 60061 - to get a fitment which had been tried and discarded many years before. In May 1958, authority was given for all the A3s to be fitted with double blastpipe and chimney. The resulting softer blast soon brought complaints of visibility impaired by smoke and steam drifting on to the front of the cab, just as happened on 2751 *HUMORIST* when it got a double chimney in 1937. Too small a volume of air resulted from this type deflector to serve any effective purpose, and other means were sought.

60098 after its final visit to Doncaster works in May 1961 shows a difference of detail such as always fascinates specialist enthusiasts, the reason for which usually proves difficult to discover. The standard position for the crossrail on the smokebox door was just above the upper hinge strap, and when the cast numberplate was put on, it was mounted immediately above the rail. 60098 was in conformity until April 1961, but then changed to a door which had a shorter crossrail above the numberplate.

2570 here on 2nd January 1928 viewed from an unusual angle, showing interesting detail. Note the different shape of reversing arm adopted for the contractor-built engines from that which Doncaster used, seen so well in the photograph of 4472 at Wembley. The absence of cab sight screen is clearly evident, as is the Westinghouse brake pump and its associated pipework. To point to the contrast in size, 2570 and Y7 class 898 (Darlington Works 0-4-0T shunter) were at a rolling stock exhibition being held at Redcar.

4481 from 1st August 1925 retained the cut-down cab roof but also the original height ventilator which showed very noticeably when seen from this angle on 10th May 1936; also clearly seen is the reduced cut-out of the cab side sheet due to fitting of bucket seat.

2553 merits mention for two items of interest. New on 31st December 1924 it was without name until into 1926 when *MANNA* plates were fitted. On 12th October 1926 in the works yard at Doncaster it was put on display for the Prince of Wales to view. This led to it being re-named *PRINCE OF WALES* from 11th November 1926, despite the LNER already having a D11 class engine carrying that name, and which it was allowed to retain. This photograph of 2553 in 1927 on a Grantham - London express also shows that it was fitted with a pyrometer connection, by then a quite rare item of equipment on A1s.

2562 was unique in two respects from its first appearance - it already had a racehorse name, but of greater importance, it carried a 62-element 'E' type superheater, which required it to be fitted with twin anti-vacuum valves behind the chimney. That was used until July 1930 but did not provide the benefit expected so was replaced by the normal type.

Reverting to normal smokebox in February 1933, 2747 left 2751 to continue efforts to solve this problem. Here at Grantham shed on 23rd August 1936, is a good view of the alteration to the cab cut-out resulting from the provision of bucket seats for the crew.

The only A1 to be disfigured by the impedimenta associated with the fitting of A.C.F.I. feed-water heating was 2576. It carried it from 30th August 1929 until going into works on 4th November 1938. The engine continued in normal service, on Gateshead shed duties. On shed at York, 2576 shows just how much this experimental apparatus ruined the clean lines of the A1 design. Benefits there were, but these were off-set by troubles keeping the proliferation of pipework from springing leaks in service.

2581 sometime between March 1930 and April 1933 had its smokebox door fastening changed to a wheel and a handle - the only such variation ever observed. This was only of short duration and was probably a 'first-aid' repair done by Heaton shed.

60057 was in the blue painting that it carried from July 1949 to October 1952 when this photograph was taken at its home shed Haymarket where it was having attention to its left steam pipe. The removal of its cover to a point further along the running plate, shows that the actual pipe was not straight but had a right-angle bend - not ideal for free steam flow.

60077 was transferred to St Margarets shed on 16th June 1963 and is seen there in August 1964. By then its livery had lost all its sheen, but this view shows the Smith-Stone speed indicator drive from the rear coupling pin. Between February 1960 and October 1962, all except five (Nos. 60055, 60064, 60079, 60095 and 60104) were so equipped following a strong hint from a Ministry of Transport Inspector's inquiry into a driver having mis-judged speed.

The second Pacific No.1471, new in July 1922, ran without a name until November 1922. Here on Sunday 3rd September 1922 it is approaching Wood Green on its way to Barkston with a 600-ton train to justify Gresley's claim as to the capability of his new design.

The higher speeds at which the streamlined trains ran caused a check to be made on the height above rail level of the centre of gravity of Pacific locomotives. In working order, this had been calculated as 5/11¼". Whilst A3 class 2598 *BLENHEIM* was in Doncaster works in October 1936 for general repair, a practical check was taken, and the actual height came out at just one sixteenth of an inch below what had been calculated, but what's the thickness of a chalk mark?

PART SIX

TRIALS & TRIBULATIONS

Gresley's Pacific design certainly provided power in plenty and was capable of being developed to do so with increasing economy at relatively small cost. The first step forward was taken in June 1925, when 4477 was altered to $\frac{3}{8}$" more steam lap in its valve setting. Here for this to be assessed it is about to depart from Doncaster station.

Further small modifications to the valve gear on 4477 were made in February 1926 and here, with indicating gear on its cylinders, it is at Potters Bar hauling the 1.30 p.m. luncheon car express from Kings Cross to Leeds, Bradford and Hull.

2751's name of *HUMORIST* proved most appropriate for the series of funny appearances which its front end underwent, in the determined attempt to solve the smoke drifting problem. Starting in April 1932, this was its initial modification. Although the front of the smokebox was cut away similarly to 2747, the air was diverted through a second chimney behind the normal one, both contained in a single casting.

2751 did further trial runs in November 1932 with a crescent shaped gap in front of the liner, but that was even less successful. In March 1933, the curved top of the smokebox was removed and these side-plates were fitted, extra vanes behind the chimney being added later. On 20th June, the Running Department said it was now satisfied that the desired result was being obtained, but not sufficiently strongly to request that others be so modified. Thus, at its next heavy repair in January 1934, 2751 reverted to normal.

The streamlined front ends of the A4 class, introduced in September 1935 proved to be the complete answer to smoke clearance, but on the A3 class it remained a problem for more than twenty years. In July 1937 trials on A3s with Kylchap double blastpipe and chimney began and 2751 again became a guinea-pig, with chimney extended forward.

The softer blast from the Kylchap arrangement quickly led to smoke drifting problems and in January 1938 a rimless chimney and longer side vanes were fitted which then gave results that could be accepted. 2751 then ran in this guise until April 1947, and by then had been re-numbered to 97.

HUMORIST in early BR livery and with full smoke deflectors. Except for minor detail alterations (lipped chimney and split smokebox door handrail) the engine ended its days in this guise.

In this 1930 picture 2582 shows off the Darlington style for the cab numbers and lettering on the tender, both on the same level but lower than put on at Doncaster.

During 1943, the new Chief Mechanical Engineer had Doncaster drawing office formulate proposals for a complete, and largely systematic, re-numbering. To show his scheme to the Directors, Thompson had photographs taken in 1944 of a range of examples carrying the initial number of the class concerned. The A3s were to begin at 500, although *CORONACH* would be 556, and it duly went back into traffic on 28th April 1944 as 2747.

PART SEVEN

LIVERIES

Faded glory - to be debited to one Adolf Hitler. 2547 *DONCASTER* named 27th March 1926 was not to honour its builders but that of the 1873 Derby winner. In April 1928 it was selected as one of the class to work the Edinburgh non-stops, and kept a corridor tender until June 1933. Here, unkempt and in plain, unlined black livery, and degraded by Thompson from A1 to A10, it has still to have L N E R restored.

60037 although displaying evidence of its new ownership acquired when ex works on 27th October 1948 had been thoroughly restored to its original livery of LNER green.

60082 photographed on 20th September 1949, was Doncaster's official record of the new blue painting with lining in black and white, and the change to British Railways' emblem.

60091 in blue, verging on purple, lined in red and cream at a rolling stock exhibition in Edinburgh Waverley station, put on for those officials concerned in the determination of British Railways' standard liveries. During May and June 1948, five other A3s were also given this style, concluded by 60036 ex works 23rd July 1948, in a lighter blue but with similar lining.

The blue painting did not suit some of the express designs which B.R. inherited, nor did it please some places where Brunswick green had always ruled. Lobbying duly had that substituted as the standard from August 1951, with orange and black lining, but the emblem survived for another six years. Of the A3 class only Nos.60070 and 60076 never had blue. 60094 got this standard green livery from 29th April 1952.

60075 *ST FRUSQUIN* is in the purple/blue painting put on ex works 28th May 1948 when B.R. were in the experimental stage regarding a standard livery. It had the unusual feature of having the red and cream lining also applied to the casing of the outside cylinders and valves.

60077 at Doncaster in July 1961 had just had trough deflectors fitted and this view clearly shows the final standard livery when newly applied. At that time it was working from sheds in the Leeds district.

The Kings Cross shedmaster Peter Townend was an enthusiastic user of the A3 class, despite their being 25 to 35 years old. Doncaster born, educated, and trained at 'The Plant', he could recall what they were capable of from the LNER's brilliant years of 1932 to 1939. Although having A4s and Peppercorn A1s at his command, he was determined, and convinced that his A3s would not be out-shone by such diesels as were being allocated to him in 1960. In true Gresley tradition, he kept a keen eye on what locomotive engineers overseas were doing, and holiday visits to Germany had shown him how effective their trough type deflectors could be. Some lobbying got an agreement that four A3s could be so fitted for practical experience to be gained on the East Coast Main Line, and 60049 *GALTEE MORE* ex works on 21st October 1960 was the first. By 18th November the Running Department were able to recommend that they be made a standard fitting on all A3s, and in March 1961 authorisation was given for all except 60097 *HUMORIST* (which did not need them as it already had large deflectors) and also the four, 60068, 60079, 60093 and 60095, at Carlisle Canal because these had become London Midland Region responsibility. Despite withdrawals having already begun and Deltics becoming available, no less than fifty five A3s acquired the trough type deflectors. 60112 changed to them in October 1962 as here 24th August 1963.

THE END

60052 still active in July 1965 when there was only one other survivor, was allocated to Edinburgh St Margarets shed, and is seen at Stonehaven, returning from Aberdeen with a train of empty coal wagons. 60052 actually went into Inverurie works for minor repairs in August 1965 and became the last of the class but was withdrawn on 17th January 1966. Along with 60041, which had been withdrawn on 4th December 1965, the pair stood outside St Margarets shed for some time afterwards. They were sold to contractors for cutting up. 60052 went in June and 60041 followed in September.

ACKNOWLEDGEMENTS

First, and most emphatically, to my wife for close on sixty years of tolerance and positive support for a hobby that she would be well justified in regarding as an obsession. Fortunately it has been leavened by giving her some firm friendships with wives of like-minded railway enthusiasts she would otherwise never have known. She has patiently provided hospitality for numerous visitors who have come to our home simply to talk about railways, LNER in particular.

Our daughter accompanied me (willingly) on more than one shed visit - Ardsley and Woodford are names that she readily recognises - and in due course had the good sense (without any prompting, because she was then 3,500 miles away) to marry a dedicated railway buff.

To offset the mass of figures in this book, which otherwise would have been intolerable, I am deeply indebted to a host of photographers who, since 1933, have enabled me to build up a collection providing evidence of almost every detail difference visible on LNER locomotives. Whilst they were still alive, I hope that I was able to make known to the following how much I appreciated their willingness to contribute their work so effectively to my collection:- Bishop Treacy, Will Whitworth, Gordon Hepburn, Douglas Stephen, Lawson Kerr, P.Ransome-Wallis, Bryce Greenfield, Ben Burrell, W.Leslie Good, George Ellis, J.J.Cunningham and Ken Hoole. To those of you who will be able to see some of your photographs included in this book, I offer a very sincere 'Thank You'.

Without the faith of Irwell Press that such a book had market viability, my L N E R locomotive knowledge would have remained largely in obscurity and known only to the *cognoscenti*.